《中国节庆文化》丛书
编委会名单

List of Members of Editorial Board
of *Chinese Festival Culture Series*

中国节庆文化丛书

Chinese Festival Culture Series

The Tibetan Calendar
New Year

主 编 李 松

副主编 张 刚 彭新良

藏历年

宋黎昀◎著

罗红云◎译

全 国 百 佳 图 书 出 版 单 位

时代出版传媒股份有限公司

安徽人民出版社

图书在版编目（CIP）数据

藏历年:汉英对照/宋黎昀著;罗红云译.—合肥:安徽人民出版社,2014.1
(中国节庆文化丛书/李松,张刚,彭新良主编)

ISBN 978－7－212－07071－7

Ⅰ.①藏…　Ⅱ.①宋…　②罗…　Ⅲ.①藏族—民族节日—中国—汉、英
Ⅳ.①K892.1

中国版本图书馆 CIP 数据核字(2013)第 315377 号

Zhongguo Jieqing Wenhua Congshu　Zanglinian
中国节庆文化丛书　藏历年

李　松　主编　张　刚　彭新良　副主编

宋黎昀　著　罗红云　译

出 版 人:朱寒冬　　　　　　　　　图书策划:胡正义　丁怀超　李　旭
责任编辑:郑世彦　方贵京　　　　　装帧设计:宋文岚

出版发行:时代出版传媒股份有限公司 http://www.press-mart.com
　　　　安徽人民出版社 http://www.ahpeople.com
　　　　合肥市政务文化新区翡翠路 1118 号出版传媒广场八楼
　　　　邮编:230071
　　　　营销部电话:0551-63533258　0551-63533292(传真)
制　　版:合肥市中旭制版有限责任公司
印　　制:安徽新华印刷股份有限公司

开本:710×1010　1/16　　　印张:12.25　　　字数:220 千
版次:2014 年 3 月第 1 版　　　2016 年 7 月第 4 次印刷

标准书号:ISBN 978－7－212－07071－7　　　定价:24.00 元

Our Common Days

(Preface)

The most important day for a person in a year is his or her birthday, and the most important days for all of us are the festivals. We can say that the festivals are our common days.

Festivals are commemorating days with various meanings. There are national, ethnic and religious festivals, such as the National Day and Christmas Day, and some festivals for certain groups, such as the Women's Day, the Children's Day and the Labor Day. There are some other festivals closely related to our lives. These festivals have long histories and different customs that have been passed on from one generation to another. There are also different traditional festivals. China is a country of 56 ethnic groups, and all of the ethnic groups are collectively called the Chinese Nation. Some traditional festivals are common to all people of the Chinese Nation, and some others are unique to certain ethnic groups. For example, the Spring Festival, the Mid-Autumn Day, the Lantern Festival, the Dragon Boat Festival, the Tomb-Sweeping Day and the Double-Ninth Day are common festivals to all of the Chinese people. On the other hand, the New Year of the Qiang Ethnic (a World Cultural Heritage), for example, is a unique festival to the Qiang Ethnic Group, and there are

我们共同的日子

（代序）

个人一年一度最重要的日子是生日，大家一年一度最重要的日子是节日。节日是大家共同的日子。

节日是一种纪念日，内涵多种多样。有民族的、国家的、宗教的，比如国庆节、圣诞节等。有某一类人的，如妇女、儿童、劳动者的，这便是妇女节、儿童节、劳动节等。也有与人们的生活生产密切相关的，这类节日历史悠久，很早就形成了一整套人们约定俗成、代代相传的节日习俗，这是一种传统的节日。传统节日也多种多样。中国是个多民族国家，有五十六个民族，统称中华民族。传统节日有全民族共有的，也有某个民族特有的。比如春节、中秋节、元宵节、端午节、清明节、重阳节等，就为中华民族所共用和共享；世界文化遗产羌年就为羌族独有和独享。各民族这样的节日很多。

传统节日是在漫长的农耕时代形成的。农耕时代生产与生活、人与自然的关系十分密切。人们或为了感恩于大自然的恩赐，或为了庆祝辛苦劳作换来的收获，或为了激发生命的活力，或为了加强人际的亲情，经过长期相互认同，最终约定俗成，渐渐把一年中某一天确定为节日，并创造了十分完整又严格的节俗，如仪式、庆典、规制、禁忌，乃至特定的游艺、装饰与食品，来把节日这天演化成一个独具内涵和迷人的日子。更重要的是，人们在每一个传统的节日里，还把共同的生活理想、人间愿望与审美追求融入节日的内涵与种种仪式中。因此，它是中华民族世间理想与生活愿望极致的表现。可以说，我们的传统——精神文化传统，往往就是依靠这代代相传的一年一度的节日继承下来的。

many festivals celebrated only by minorities in China.

The traditional festivals are formed throughout the long agrarian age, during which the relationships between life and production and between the people and the nature were very close. To express the gratitude to the nature for its gifts, or celebrate the harvests from hard works, or stimulate the vitality of life, or strengthen the relationships among people, people would determine one day in a year as a festival with complete and strict customs, such as ceremonies, rules and taboos, special activities, decorations and foods to make the festival a day with unique meanings and charms. More importantly, people would integrate their good wishes into the meanings and ceremonies of the festivals. Therefore, the festivals could represent the ideals and wishes of the people in the best way. It is safe to say that our traditions, more specifically, our spiritual and cultural traditions, are inherited through the festivals year by year.

However, since the 20th century, with the transition from the agricultural civilization to the industrial civilization, the cultural traditions formed during the agrarian age have begun to collapse. Especially in China, during the process of opening up in the past 100 years, the festival culture, especially the festival culture in cities, has been impacted by the modern civilization and foreign cultures. At present, the Chinese people have felt that the traditional festivals are leaving away day by day so that some worries are produced about this. With the diminishing of the traditional festivals, the traditional spirits carried by them will also disappear. However, we are not just watching them disappearing, but actively dealing with them, which could fully represent the self-consciousness of the Chinese people in terms of culture.

In those ten years, with the fully launching of the folk culture heritage rescue program of China, and the promotion of the application for national immaterial cultural heritage list, more attention has been paid to the traditional festivals, some of which have been added to the central cultural heritage list. After that, in 2006, China has determined that the second Saturday of June of each year shall be the Cultural Heritage Day, and in 2007, the State Council added three important festivals, namely the Tomb-sweeping Day, the Dragon Boat Festival and the Mid-Autumn Day, as the legal holidays. These decisions have showed that our government

然而，自从二十世纪整个人类进入了由农耕文明向工业文明的过渡，农耕时代形成的文化传统开始瓦解。尤其是中国，在近百年由封闭走向开放的过程中，节日文化——特别是城市的节日文化受到现代文明与外来文化的冲击。当下人们已经鲜明地感受到传统节日渐行渐远，并为此产生忧虑。传统节日的淡化必然使其中蕴含的传统精神随之涣散。然而，人们并没有坐等传统的消失，主动和积极地与之应对。这充分显示了当代中国人在文化上的自觉。

近十年，随着中国民间文化遗产抢救工程的全面展开，国家非物质文化遗产名录申报工作的有力推动，传统节日受到关注，一些重要的传统节日列入了国家文化遗产名录。继而，2006年国家将每年六月的第二个周六确定为"文化遗产日"；2007年国务院决定将三个中华民族的重要节日——清明节、端午节和中秋节列为法定放假日。这一重大决定，表现了国家对公众的传统文化生活及其传承的重视与尊重，同时也是保护节日文化遗产十分必要的措施。

节日不放假必然直接消解了节日文化，放假则是恢复节日传统的首要条件。但放假不等于远去的节日立即就会回到身边。节日与假日的不同是因为节日有特定的文化内容与文化形式。那么，重温与恢复已经变得陌生的传统节日习俗则是必不可少的了。

千百年来，我们的祖先从生活的愿望出发，为每一个节日都创造出许许多多美丽又动人的习俗。这种愿望是理想主义的，所以节日习俗是理想的；愿望是情感化的，所以节日习俗也是情感化的；愿望是美好的，所以节日习俗是美的。人们用合家团聚的年夜饭迎接新年；把天上的明月化为手中甜甜的月饼，来象征人间的团圆；在严寒刚刚消退、万物复苏的早春，赶到野外去打扫墓地，告慰亡灵，

emphasizes and respects the traditional cultural activities and their heritages. Meanwhile, these are important measures to protect festival cultural heritages.

Festivals without holidays will directly harm the festival culture. Holiday is the most important condition for the recovery of a festival, but holiday does not mean that the festival will come back immediately. Festivals are different from holidays because festivals have unique cultural contents and forms. Therefore, it will be necessary to review and recover the customs of the traditional festivals that have become strange to us.

For thousands of years, our ancestors created beautiful and moving customs for each festival based on their best wishes. The customs are ideal, since the wishes are ideal. The customs are emotional, since the wishes are emotional. The customs are beautiful, since the wishes are beautiful. We have the family reunion dinner to receive a new year. We make moon cakes according to the shape of the moon in the mid-autumn to symbolize the reunion of our family. We visit the tombs of our ancestors in the early spring and go outing to beautiful and green hills to express our grief. These beautiful festival customs have offered us great comfort and peace for generations.

To ethnic minorities, their unique festivals are of more importance, since these festivals bear their common memories and represent their spirits, characters and identities.

Who ever can say that the traditional customs are out of date? If we have forgotten these customs, we should review them. The review is not imitating the customs of our ancients, but experiencing the spirits and emotions of the traditions with our heart.

During the course of history, customs are changing, but the essence of the national tradition will not change. The tradition is to constantly pursue a better life, to be thankful to the nature and to express our best wishes for family reunion and the peace of the world.

This is the theme of our festivals, and the reason and purpose of this series of books.

The planning and compiling of the series is unique. All of the festivals are held once a year. Since China is a traditional agricultural society,

表达心中的缅怀，同时戴花插柳，踏青春游，亲切地拥抱大地山川……这些诗意化的节日习俗，使我们一代代人的心灵获得了美好的安慰与宁静。

对于少数民族来说，他们特有的节日的意义则更加重要。节日还是他们民族集体记忆的载体、共同精神的依托、个性的表现、民族身份之所在。

谁说传统的习俗过时了？如果我们淡忘了这些习俗，就一定要去重温一下传统。重温不是表象地模仿古人的形式，而是用心去体验传统中的精神与情感。

在历史的进程中，习俗是在不断变化的，但民族传统的精神本质不应变。这传统就是对美好生活不懈的追求，对大自然的感恩与敬畏，对家庭团圆与世间和谐永恒的企望。

这便是我们节日的主题，也是这套节庆丛书编写的根由与目的。

这套书的筹划独具匠心。所有节日都是一年一次。由于我国为传统农耕社会，所以生活与生产同步，节日与大自然的节气密切相关。本丛书以一年的春、夏、秋、冬四个时间板块，将纷繁的传统节日清晰有序地排列开来，又总揽成书，既包括全民族共有的节日盛典，也把少数民族重要的节日遗产纳入其中，以周详的文献和生动的传说，将每个节日的源起、流布与习俗，亦图亦文、有滋有味地娓娓道来。一节一册，单用方便，放在一起则是中华民族传统节日的一部全书，既有知识性、资料性、工具性，又有阅读性和趣味性。这样一套丛书不仅是对我国传统节日的一次总结，也是对传统节日文化富于创意的弘扬。

　　我读了书稿，心生欣喜，因序之。

冯骥才

2013.12.25

the life is synchronized with production, and the festivals are closely relevant to the climates. In this series, all of the traditional festivals in China will be introduced in the order of the four seasons, covering the common festivals as well as important ethnic festivals that have been listed as cultural heritages. All of the festivals are described in detail with texts and images to introduce their origins, customs and distribution. Each book of the series is used to introduce one festival so that it is convenient to read individually and it may be regarded as a complete encyclopedia if connected with each other. Therefore, it is not only intellectual, informative and instrumental, but also readable and interesting. The series could be used as a tool book or read for leisure. It is not only the summary of the traditional festivals of our country, but an innovative promotion of our traditional festival culture.

I felt very delighted after reading the manuscript, so I wrote this preface.

Feng Jicai

December 25th, 2013

目　录 / Contents

第一章

藏历年的历史

除旧迎新，祈福来年，这恐怕是全人类对新年寄予的共同深切愿望。新年对各民族来说几乎都是一年当中最重要的节日。同样的，对藏族来说，藏历新年也是他们在一年当中最热闹、最隆重的日子。藏区各地在藏历新年的时候都会举行各种庆祝活动和仪式来迎接新的一年，希望来年幸福、好运，家人健康，庄稼丰收，等等。藏历年从它诞生之日到今天已有上千年的历史，在千年历史的流转当中，藏历年作为一种年节习俗也不断丰富其内涵，形成了今天这样一个不仅文化内涵丰富而且深具藏地文化特色的节日庆典，越来越被世界各地人民所喜爱和瞩目。该书希望以绵薄之力尽量将藏历年的文化内涵全面呈现给读者。虽然藏历年是藏地人民普遍都会进行的最隆重的年节庆典，但由于藏区各地历史、地理和经济条件、风土人情的不同，藏历年的庆祝方式存在很强烈的地区差异。在该书的介绍中，由于篇幅所限，也不能面面俱到，因此笔者考虑大致以拉萨地区的藏历年为主要介绍对象，再兼具其他几个主要不同的藏区的情况，希望能尽量全面而不失重点。

Chapter One

History of the Tibetan New Year

The common and deep wish of the human being for New Year is to send off the old year and usher in the new and pray for the following year. As for all ethnic groups, New Year is almost the most important festival in a year. Similarly, Tibetan New Year is the grandest and liveliest day in a year for Tibetans. Various kinds of celebration activities and ceremonies are held all over Tibet during the Tibetan New Year, and Tibetans wish happiness, good luck, family health, harvest, etc. for the following year. Since the making of the Tibetan calendar, it has had a history of over a thousand years till now, enriched its connotation constantly as a festival convention, formed such a festival celebration with rich cultural connotation and profound Tibetan cultural characteristics in the circulation of the history of a thousand years and attracted worldwide attention. The book tries its best to fully present the cultural connotation of the Tibetan calendar to readers. Although the Tibetan calendar is the grandest festival celebration for Tibetans, the celebration methods of the Tibetan calendar differ greatly in regions because of different historical, geographic and economic conditions in Tibetan areas. The book cannot explain everything in the short introduction, so it mainly focuses on the Tibetan calendar in Lhasa region and also takes into considerations different situations in other Tibetan areas in order to comprehensively analyze the traditions.

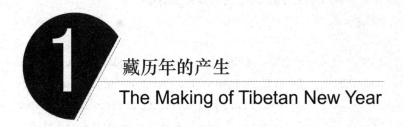

藏历年的产生
The Making of Tibetan New Year

Tibetan New Year wasn't a festival celebration at the very beginning, and its making experienced a long historical evolution, and the making and evolution of the Tibetan calendar algorithm played a key role in the founding of Tibetan New Year during this evolution. At present, there is a comparatively homogeneous Tibetan New Year in Tibetan areas, but they are mainly differentiated in various regions in terms of time. Different regions in Tibet adopt different dates for the Tibetan calendar, for example, the first day of the first month of the Tibetan calendar is Tibetan New Year in Lhasa; Gongbo forest area in the east of Lhasa celebrates New Year on the first day of the tenth month rather than the first day of the first month of the Tibetan calendar; some places in Qamdo celebrate New Year on the first day of the eleventh month, and some counties and cities in other Tibetan areas even have different Tibetan New Year dates sometimes. The great

　　藏历年并不是一个一开始就存在的年节庆典，它的产生是经过一个漫长的历史演变，在这个演变中，藏族历法的产生和演变是致使藏历年诞生的关键因素。在今天的藏区，虽然大致已有一个相对统一的藏历年，但各地还是有比较明显的差异，这个差异首先就体现在时间上。藏区各地过藏历年的时间还不尽统一，譬如拉萨是以藏历的正月初一为藏历新年；而拉萨东部的工布森林地区并不是藏历的正月初一过年，而是在藏历十月初一过年；昌都的一些地方则以十一月一日为新年，其他藏区各地甚至各县市的藏历年在时间上有时候也存在差异。今天藏历年在时间上的不同，就跟它的起源以及藏历历法的演变有很大的关系。

相传，藏族的历法约开始于公元前一百年，是由前藏雅隆地方一个叫作噶莫帕玛的人根据月亮的圆缺初步推算出了日、月、年，是一个比较简单的历算法，人们把这个历法叫《噶莫帕玛历算法》。后来由于该地区农业的发展，每当庄稼成熟并收获一次后，人们便要举行一次聚会庆祝丰收，年复一年，这种活动就慢慢形成了定期庆祝，后来人们就习惯以庄稼成熟为一年的开始。《旧唐书吐蕃传》内记："不知节候，以麦熟为岁首。"《新唐书吐蕃传》内也说："其四时，以麦熟为岁首。"因此，大概在唐代以前，藏族是以麦熟为新年，所以他们过年往往不是在冬春之交，而是在初秋或者深秋过年。现在在藏区的某些地方，在青稞黄熟的时候会过一年一

difference of Tibetan New Year in terms of time today is largely related to the origin and evolution of the Tibetan calendar algorithm.

It's said that the Tibetan calendar began around 100 B.C., a man called Gamo Pama calculated the day, month and year according to the wax and wane of the moon preliminarily in the place of Yalong in Anterior Tibet, which was a simple calendar algorithm and was called *Gamo Pama Calendar Algorithm*. Later, people held a party to celebrate a bumper harvest after harvesting crops with the development of agriculture in this area, this kind of activity had gradually turned into periodical celebration year after year, and people were accustomed to adopting the ripening of crops as the beginning of a year. *History of Tibet in the Old Book of Tang* recorded that it didn't know seasons and climate and used the ripening of wheat as the beginning of a year. *History of Tibet in the New Book of Tang* recorded that it had four seasons and used the ripening of wheat as the beginning of a year. Therefore, Tibetans used the ripening of wheat as New Year before the Tang Dynasty, and they usually celebrated New Year in early or deep fall rather than at the end of winter and the beginning of spring. At present, some regions in Tibet celebrate the annual "Ongkor Festival" for harvest when highland barley ripens; the places in Gongbo Area including Nyingchi celebrate New Year on the first day of the tenth month of the Tibetan calendar after the harvest of wheat, and it's said that it is the proof of the convention of "using the harvest of wheat as the beginning of a year" in ancient Tibet. It's said that there were seven types of the beginning of a year in Tibet in ancient times, and were equal to the months of the Han lunar calendar respectively:

Kalachakra Tantra: The first day of the third month is the beginning of a year;

Four Tantras: The first day of the first month is the beginning of a year;

Four Sutras: The first day of the twelfth month is the beginning of a year;

Interpretation of Five Elements: The first day of the eleventh month is the beginning of a year;

Kosha: The sixteenth day of the seventh month is the beginning of a year;

Sun Sutra: The sixteenth day of the ninth month is the beginning of a year;

Retribution Sutra Interpretation: The sixteenth day of the eighth month is the beginning of a year.

Latter, Tibetan people absorbed cultures of other places including astronomy and calendar in the process of the historical development, and they mastered calendars from other places and created their own calendar system. It was said that Tibet was influenced by the Chinese calendar algorithm which was brought by Princess Wencheng in the Zhenguan period of Tang Dynasty, which played a very important role in improving and developing the

度的"望果节"，庆贺庄稼丰收；工布藏区林芝等地的藏历年之所以是在藏历十月初一麦子丰收后过年，据说就是藏地古时以"麦收为岁首"的习俗在现今的见证。在远古时代的西藏，据说岁首有七种，分别相当于汉地农历的月份是：

时轮经：三月初一为岁首；

四部医典：正月初一为岁首；

四座经：十二月初一为岁首；

五行释者：十一月初一为岁首；

俱舍论：七月十六为岁首；

日藏经：九月十六为岁首；

因缘经释：八月十六为岁首。

后来，在历史的发展过程中，藏地不断吸收其他地方的文化，包括天文历法，藏地将各地的历法融会贯通，慢慢形成自己的一套历法系统。其中对藏地影响最大的据说是唐贞观年间，文成公主入藏将汉地的历算法带到西藏，对藏历的完善和发展起了极其重要的作用，这时计算新年的第一天的方法已从月亮的圆缺进步到以星辰为主要依据，但仍以现藏历的十一月一日为新年。到公元1027年，也就是宋仁宗天圣五年，印度的时轮历法传入西藏，西藏的历法遂逐步形成了以汉地农历、印度时轮历法和藏地古老历法相结合的藏历，到了八思巴（公元1235－1280年）的萨迦派统治全藏时，藏历已完全成熟，过年的仪式也基本固定下来，一直沿袭到今天。藏历从元代开始即确定一年为十二个月，大月三十天，小月二十九天，每一千日左右，便有一个闰月，用来调整月份和季节的关系。其纪年虽然不用汉历的干支，但能和汉历干支吻合，它是用金、木、水、火、土五行配搭于十二地支属相之上来纪年，如金鼠、金牛、火虎、火兔等，而若查汉族农历，可发现甲子乙丑为金，丙寅丁卯为火，子为鼠，丑为牛，寅为

Tibetan calendar, and the method calculating the first day of New Year had progressed from the waxing and waning of the moon to the observations of stars at that time, but the first day of the eleventh month in the Tibetan calendar was still adopted as New Year. Till A.D.1027, i.e., the fifth year of Tiansheng Reign of Emperor Renzong in the Song Dynasty, Indian Kalachakra calendar was introduced into Tibet, and then the Tibetan calendar had gradually formed into the calendar integrating Chinese lunar calendar, Indian Kalachakra calendar and ancient Tibetan calendar. The Tibetan calendar had grown maturely till Basiba (1235—1280) which was dominated by Sakya School in Tibet. The ceremony celebrating New Year had been fixed basically, and it has been followed today. Since the beginning of the Yuan Dynasty, the Tibetan calendar has been confirmed that there are twelve months in a year, thirty days in a big month, and twenty-nine days in a small month, and there is an intercalary month for about one thousand days, which is used to adjust the relationship between months and seasons. Although its calendar doesn't adopt Chinese heavenly stems and earthly branches, it matches with them and counts years by matching the five elements of gold, wood, water, fire and earth with the twelve earthly branches, such as gold rat, gold ox, fire tiger and fire rabbit etc. We can find that Jia-zi and Yi-chou are gold, Bing-yin and Ding-mao are fire, Zi is rat, Chou is ox, Yin is tiger, Mao is rabbit and so on. If there is Jia-zi year, it can be called gold rat year in the Tibetan calendar, and Yi-chou year can be called as gold ox year in the Tibetan calendar, so the structure of the Tibetan calendar is similar to Chinese calendar. Every sixty years is a great cycle, and is called *raoqiong*. The first *raoqiong* began from A.D.1027, so a more mature Tibetan calendar formed in A.D.1027 basically. The local Tibetan regime began to confirm that the first day of the first month was the Tibetan calendar since 1027. However, Tibetans avoid many days which are seen as taboos, that is to say, they tell fortunes of days, eliminate a terrible day when they make the calendar, choose the previous or latter lucky day to repeat a day, for example, if the fifteenth day is a terrible day, it will be eliminated, and the fourteenth or the sixteenth day will be repeated. In Tibetan-inhabited areas, people believe that the first, the third and the fifteenth days are unfortunate days.They will not make a pilgrimage or pray to gods on these days, and they will be eliminated in the calendar[1]. Therefore, Tibetan New Year is celebrated on different days in Tibetan areas each year.

虎，卯为兔，等等。若是甲子年，藏历亦可称为金鼠年，乙丑年藏历亦可为金牛年，所以藏历的组织跟汉历是相似的。每六十年为一周，一大循环，称为一个"饶琼"。第一个"饶琼"就是从公元1027年开始，所以基本上在1027年形成了一个比较成熟的藏历。当时的西藏地方政权从1027年开始确定藏历正月初一为藏历年。但是，因为藏人对日子多有忌讳，即会占卜日子的吉凶，造历书的时候会将大凶之日削去，而选一个之前或之后比较吉利的日子重复一日，譬如若15日为大凶日则削去15日，重复14日或者16日。在康藏地区，人们一般相信各月的1、3、15等日为不祥日，在这些日子不朝山敬神，历书中也每每将这些日子削去[1]。因此，在藏区，每年过藏历年的时间都有可能不同。

[1]Refer to Ren Naiqiang, *Xikang Illustrations: Folk Custom*, p.320, collected by *A Collection of Ren Naiqiang on the Tibetan Studies*, China Tibetology Publishing House, 2002.

[1]参见任乃强《西康图经·民俗篇》320页，收于《任乃强藏学文集·上册》中国藏学出版社2002年版。

藏历年的历史与传承
History and Inheritance of Tibetan New Year

除了在过年时间上的不同和地区习俗上的差异，藏历年在一千多年的传承里面随着时代的变迁也多少打上了不同时代的烙印。特别在1959年以前，达赖喇嘛统治时期的西藏，藏历年跟现在有很多差别，那时由于掌权的是僧侣阶层，因此藏历年有更加浓厚的藏传佛教色彩。在当时社会等级分明的状况下，喇嘛阶层、俗官阶层和一般老百姓过藏历年都有不同的庆贺方式。而如今的西藏，藏人过藏历年已没有那么明显的等级区划，而是有更加浓厚的娱乐化和市民化色

Besides the differences of time of celebrating New Year and local conventions, Tibetan New Year has been etched by marks of different eras in the ever-changing process of inheritance and transition over one thousand years. Particularly, Tibetan New Year differed greatly from the present one before 1959 in Tibet in the domination of Dalai Lama, which was controlled by the monk class, so Tibetan New Year had strong influence of Tibetan Buddhism. In the conditions of the strict social hierarchy, Lama class, secular official class and common people had different celebration methods at that time. At present, there aren't clear distinctions for Tibetans to celebrate Tibetan New Year in Tibet, but the celebrations become more entertaining and popularized. In the record of some historical literatures, we can reminisce the scenes that Tibetan New Year was celebrated in the old Tibet:

"Tibetans in different classes celebrated New Year at different times. Peasants began to celebrate New Year in the first half of the twelfth month, and temples held holy ceremonies in the latter half of the month; when New Year approached, every Tibetan looked forward to celebration and parades, and there were full of activities."

"Tibetans liked taking part in merriment, they will not miss fights on streets or in grand parades, and 'Te-Mo' was named to this inclination and also became the name of a big festival. Devils dance was played in Potala on the twenty-ninth day of the twelfth month in the Tibetan calendar, which was the prelude of Te-Mo."

"Usually, people played devil-driving dance on the brond stone square in the east of Potala Palace. The delicate Lama band which was composed of drummers and trumpeters accompanied under the direction of a cymbal player and nearly fifty artists who dressed up performed this serious religious ceremony drama, which was a story about Buddhism and monks with black hat who protected gods and punished devils. There was a painting among props, on which there was a devil suffering in an oil boiler. A Grand Lama poured a glass of liquor to the

彩。在一些历史文献的记载中，我们可以看到旧时西藏过藏历年的一些情形：

"不同阶层的西藏人在不同的时间过新年。藏历十二月的上半月，农民开始庆贺新年；下半月寺庙举行神圣的庆典；然后新年来临，随之而来的是每个藏人期盼的庆祝和游行，节目排得满满的。"

"藏人最喜欢凑热闹，无论是街头的打斗还是大游行都不放过，并为此得名'代莫'（Te-Mo），这还成为一个大节日的名称。藏历十二月二十九日在布达拉跳打鬼舞（面具舞 Devils Dance），这是代莫的序曲。"

"一般是在布达拉宫东侧的一个宽阔的石头广场上跳打鬼舞。鼓手和号手组成别致的喇嘛乐队，在一个击镲人的指挥下伴奏，约五十名精心打扮的艺人演出这场严肃的宗教仪式剧，这是一个关于佛教和黑帽僧人的保护神惩罚恶魔的故事。道具中有一幅画，画上是一个正在油锅里煎熬的恶魔。一位大喇嘛突然将一杯酒泼向这幅画，这幅画被点燃，射向天空变成一柱烟火，这是表演的高潮。据说这些演员都来自达赖的私庙，面具和戏装都是在北京定做的。"

"新年的头三天，拉萨人停止一切商贸活动庆贺新年。布达拉宫每天早上都有庆祝仪式，大家分别敬贺达赖喇嘛的三种不同身份：第一天，作为宗教领袖；第二天，政治领袖；第三天，佛教保护神。我们已经在前面的章节里详细描述了第一天活动的过程。第二天的仪式基本相似，只是俗人角色更为突出，还要举行新任政府官员的就职仪式，这是每年三次中的第一次。"

"（新年）第二天的仪式有一个有趣的表演。布达拉宫的下方竖起一个高高的杆子，一个来自后藏的选手要攀登到杆子顶部一块旋转的板子上，做出一些滑稽的动作供大家取乐。据老一代人回忆，

painting suddenly. The painting fired, flied into the sky and became flame, which was the climax of the performance. It was said that the actors came from private temples of Dalai, and the masks and stage costumes were customized in Beijing."

"During the first three days of New Year, Lhasa people stopped all business and trade activities to celebrate New Year. There were celebration ceremonies on every morning in the Potala Palace, and they offered congratulations to three different identities of Dalai Lama: on the first day, religious leader; on the second day, political leader; on the third day, protective god of Buddhism. The processes of the activities on the first day had been described in detail in the previous section. The ceremonies on the second day were similar basically, while secular role was more outstanding, and inauguration of new governmental officials was held, which was the first inauguration among three ones."

"There was a funny performance in the ceremonies on the second day (of New Year). There was a high pole in the ground of the Potala Palace, and a player from Tsang climbed onto the rotational plate at the top of the pole and entertained people with funny actions. According to the memory of the old generation, this player usually sat on a piece of wooden saddle, which was bound with a rope he slid from another rope from the top of the Potala center to the ground, there was a distance of three hundred feet, and many people fell to death or were hurt because of friction between wooden saddle and rope during the period of the Thirteenth Dalai. After the Thirteenth Dalai put a ban on it, it had turned into this method which is more light-hearted at present. It was said that Tsang people were forced to serve in order to expand the Potala Palace. They built the top of Red Palace larger than its bottom, which looked like an upside-down pagoda. Sung-GyeGyam-Tsho, who was the then regent, was angry, and stipulated that Tsang people designated a representative to slide from the dangerous top of Red Palace as the punishment each year."

"On the third day of New Year, the last and most important flag-pole was erected in Lhasa, which safeguarded the political fate of Tibet. Clerical and secular officials administrating Lhasa city supervised the whole process on the site. Once the flag-pole was erected, they rode horses to report to Dalai in the Potala Palace. Meanwhile, it was time to begin the ceremony which celebrated Dalai Lama as the protective god of Buddhism. Since the fourth day of Tibetan New Year, there were six holy meals each

十三世达赖时期，这名选手常常坐在一块木鞍上，木鞍捆在一条绳子上，他从布达拉中心的最高处，沿着另一条绳子滑到地面，上下的落差有三百英尺，许多人被摔死或因木鞍与绳索摩擦着火而受伤。十三世达赖喇嘛下令禁止后，才换成如今这种相对轻松的方式。据说，第五世达赖喇嘛时期，为了扩建布达拉宫，后藏人被迫来此服役。他们故意把红宫的顶部建得大于底部，就像一个倒置的佛塔。当时的摄政桑结嘉措（Sung-GyeGyam-Tsho）因此大怒，规定每年派一名后藏人为代表，从红宫的顶部危险地下滑作为惩罚。"

"新年的第三天，拉萨竖起了最重要的也是最后的一根旗杆，它护卫着西藏的政治命运。管理拉萨市的僧俗官员都要到场监督整个过程。一旦旗杆竖起，他们立刻策马去布达拉宫向达赖汇报。这时，也只能在这时才开始祝贺达赖喇嘛作为佛教保护神的仪式。从藏历新年的第四天开始，每天要吃六顿圣餐：三顿'稀'（饮茶），三顿'干'。格鲁派的大住持甘丹墀巴主持早上的第一顿饭。三顿干饭期间，一级神学博士与所有挑战者公开辩论。三顿稀饭（饮茶）之后，在大昭寺各个殿前向僧众发布施。"

day, including three (tea) 'drinks' and three 'dry' meals. Ganden Thripa, the Grand Abbot of Gelug Sect held the first meal in the morning. During the three dry meals, supreme theological doctors will debate with all challengers openly. After the three (tea) drinks, alms were given to monks in the halls of the palaces of the Jokhang Temple."

1. Tibetan New Year of Dalai Lama and the Monk Class in Old Times

Tibetan New Year in Lhasa, especially a series of ceremonies which centered on Dalai Lama and the monk class in the Potala Palace during the domination period of Dalai Lama, cannot be seen in Tibet at present. However, we can know the conditions of Tibetan New Year which was celebrated in Lhasa, especially the profile of ceremonies held in the Potala Palace from many historical literatures at that time, including records of missionaries and foreign travelers entering into Tibet. As the most authoritative leader in the old times, he often held some particular ceremonies on New Year's Day in the Potala Palace:

"The conch was blown at the top of the Potala Palace when the morning star rose on the first day of the first month in the Tibetan calendar. With the care of the attendants, Dalai Lama got up from the bed, entered Gaden Shartse Hall, had breakfast with the care of pantry khenpo and bedchamber khenpo, presented treasury Hada and five kinds of offerings to the Thangka portrait of the Glorious Goddess Palden Lhamo of Gendun Gyatso who was the Second Dalai Lama, prayed to the Glorious Goddess and made New Year vows."

一、旧时达赖喇嘛及僧侣阶层的藏历年

在达赖喇嘛统治时期，拉萨的藏历年，特别在布达拉宫会有一系列以达赖喇嘛和僧侣阶层为中心的仪式，这些仪式在今天的西藏已经不太能看到。但是我们可以从过去的许多历史文献包括进入藏区的传教士和外国旅行者的记录中一窥当时拉萨过藏历年的情况，特别是在布达拉宫举行仪式的大概状况。达赖喇嘛作为旧时西藏拥有最高权威的领袖，在新年之际的布达拉宫内会进行一些特殊的仪式：

"藏历正月初一，当启明星升起的时候，布达拉宫宫顶便吹响吉祥的螺号。达赖喇嘛在侍从们的照料下，从睡榻起来，进入甘丹央孜宫，在司膳堪布和侍寝堪布的照应下，进食早餐，然后向二世达赖喇嘛根敦嘉措的本尊神吉祥天女班丹拉姆的唐卡画像敬献内库哈达和五种供品，并向吉祥天女祈祷，发新年祝愿。"

"当太阳照到布达拉宫金顶的时候，僧俗官员们迎请达赖喇嘛到红宫的顶层，那里设有达赖的宝座，他按惯例要向三届主母吉祥天女抛掷、敬献朵玛施食。接着在噶伦、近侍和僧俗官员们的簇拥下，进入白宫司西平措（圆满有寂）大殿，参加盛大的藏历新年庆典，藏话叫'噶卓'。这时驻藏大臣和达赖喇嘛互献内库哈达，互祝新年吉祥如意。摄政、噶伦等原西藏地方政府僧俗官员，还有哲蚌寺、色拉寺的上师堪布，依次向达赖喇嘛致敬并献三次哈达，参加庆典的来宾归位落座。布达拉宫宫廷乐舞队的舞童十余人，身穿五彩衣，头戴白布圈，靴上系满铃铛，上场跳钺斧舞，歌词是：'殊胜布达拉宫，殿宇金碧辉煌，胜幢五彩飞扬。'人们献上酥糕、酥油茶、人参果、甜米饭、油炸面点、各类水果，等等。三大寺两位经典娴熟，口才敏捷的高僧，当

"When the sun shone the golden top of the Potala Palace, clerical and secular officials welcomed Dalai Lama to the top of Red Palace, where there was the throne for Dalai. Dalai Lama threw and offered Duoma to the Glorious Goddess who was the matron of the three Dalais. Attended by Galoins, attendants and clerical and secular officials, he entered the West Chamber of Sunshine (Parinirvana) of the White Palace, took part in grand celebration of Tibetan New Year, which was called 'Gazhuo' in Tibetan. Meanwhile, Grand Resident Minister in Tibet and Dalai Lama presented royal treasury Hadas mutually, and wished a happy New Year and luck each other. Former local governmental clerical and secular officials in Tibet including the regent, Galoins, Guru Khenpos of the Drepung Temple and the Salad Temple paid their respects to Dalai Lama and presented Hadas thrice in turn, and guests participating in celebration were seated. There were over ten dancing children of the dancing team of the Potala Palace wore five-colored garments with white-cloth circles on heads and bells on boots, they played battle axe dance, and sang the song saying that 'the extraordinary Potala Palace had splendid and magnificent temples and halls, which were filled with five colors'. People offered Su cake, ghee tea, Ginseng fruit, sweet rice, fried pastes and various kinds of fruits etc. Two distinguished monks of the three temples with mature skills and agile eloquence debated on classics on the site. Dalai Lama laid his hand on the top of head of each participant and made wishes for New Year. Fritters were thrown and grabbed, and the celebration was completed in the festival mood. On the third day of the first month of the Tibetan calendar, the first important thing in the Potala Palace was that Dalai Lama paid religious homage to the Glorious Goddess Palden Lhamo, and asked for fortunes for that year in the way of Zanba divination. The divination was asked in this way: firstly, whether the Great Emperor was lucky, safe and sound; secondly, whether Dalai and Panchen went on well in the year; thirdly, whether all the administration policies in Tibetan local governments were adequate; and fourthly, whether common people in the snow region were happy and lived peacefully."

Besides various kinds of ceremonies which were held by Dalai Lama in the Potala Palace, there were diversified meetings and ceremonies which were held by the grand temples to celebrate Tibetan New Year, and the Lama class showed their absolute authority in Tibet at this moment through these ceremonies and meetings, and the most important one was Grand New Year Wish-making Ceremony.

Since the third or fourth day of New Year, Lhasa began to hold New Year Wish-making Ceremony, which was called Prayer Ceremony or "Molang Qinbo" in Tibetan.It was a praying ceremony of Buddhists from the third or fourth day to the twenty-

场进行经学辩论。达赖喇嘛为每一位参加庆典的人摩顶，进行新年祝福。最后撒卡色（油炸果）、抢卡色，在一片节日的欢乐中庆典结束。藏历正月初三，布达拉宫里第一件大事是达赖喇嘛再次朝拜吉祥天女班丹拉姆，通过糌粑团问卜的方式，卜问本年的吉凶福祸。问卜往往这样进行：一问大皇帝本年是否平安；二问达赖和班禅本年是否一切顺利；三问西藏地方政府一切施政是否得当；四问雪域僧俗百姓本年是否康乐。"

除了达赖喇嘛在布达拉宫内进行的各种特别仪式，在旧时西藏，过藏历年的时候各大寺院的法会仪式特别繁多，喇嘛阶层也通过这些仪式法会在这个时刻显示出他们在西藏的绝对权威。其中最为重要的就是新年大祈愿法会。

从新年的第三天或者第四天开始，拉萨会举行新年大祈愿法会，又叫传召法会，藏语是"莫郎木钦慕"，是教徒们的祈祷法会，从藏历元月三四日至二十五日，这也是拉萨的僧侣阶层每年过年举行的最重要、最盛大的宗教法会，拉萨三大寺的僧人集会寺中，西藏各地的僧俗群众也络绎不绝，蜂拥而至。这是一次不分教派，不分地区的佛教徒的大集会。传召会期间，一切权力归哲蚌寺的铁棒僧人接管。因此，传召会与其说是向佛陀祈愿不如说是向众生显示神威，是藏传佛教一年一度的大示威活动。从当时一些访藏人士的记录当中，我们也可以很明显地感受到僧侣阶层在新年祈愿大会上的权威气势：

"新年大祈愿法会从藏历新年的第三天开始，一早就人声鼎沸。哲蚌寺的铁棒喇嘛要带着他们的头陀（僧兵）来维持秩序，这时的拉萨处于戒严状态。一般是在午前，哲蚌寺的铁棒喇嘛及成群的信徒穿着华丽的大袍，骑着挂着铃铛的马匹，风卷残云般地冲进城市，俨然一副征服者的神态。他们

fifth day of the first month in the Tibetan calendar as well as the most important and grandest religious ceremony held by the Lhasa monk class each year. The monks of the three Lhasa temples got together in the temples. Monks and common people all over Tibet came and crowded there. This was the grand assembly of Buddhists without distinctions of sects or locations. During the prayer ceremony, the iron-rod monks took over all authorities of the Drepung Temple. Therefore, the Prayer Ceremony was an annual grand demonstration activity of Tibetan Buddhism which demonstrated invincible might to all living creatures rather than praying to Buddhas. From records of some persons visiting Tibet at that time, we can obviously feel the authoritative momentum of the monk class on New Year Wish-making Ceremony:

"Grand New Year Wish-making Ceremony began from the third day of Tibetan New Year, and there was a hubbub of voices. The iron-rod Lamas in the Drepung Temple brought the monk warriors to maintain order, and Lhasa was in the state of curfew at that time. Usually in the morning, the iron-rod Lamas and followers in groups wearing splendid gowns in the Drepung Temple rode horses with bells, and charged into the city quickly with the manner of conqueror. They cried to report their coming, scolded passengers on both sides to dodge fast, rode a cycle of Eight Barkhor (Middle

Ring) conqueringly, then lodged their tents at a corner near the Jokhang Temple, and performed their holy function to safeguard Lhasa for twenty-one days. The fifth Dalai Lama was the former Lama of the Drepung Temple, he preferred to this temple naturally, once issued the special order, and designated the Lamas in the Drepung Temple to take responsibility for social security of Lhasa during Grand Wish-making Ceremony. This special mission made the Lamas in the Drepung Temple become overwhelmingly arrogant. When they began to implement the mission, they held a funny ceremony. When the iron-rod Lama was sworn in, he designated other two representatives to dress up as him with the iron rods (which symbolized power) and declared their power to the mass. Guided by the strong and tall attendants with whip rods in their hands, the two representatives came to the gate of Lhasa government. The gate of the government was closed, the former guards had been withdrawn, twelve governmental clerks stood in rows, and each row had four persons, who had hats in their hands, bowed behind a smoking wood stack, and listened to their instructions respectfully. The two representatives stood out in turn, gave instructions in resonant voice very arrogantly and dramatically, reminded these governmental officials that safeguarding order of Lhasa during the Grand Prayer Ceremony was the sole authority of the Lamas of the Drepung Temple, and warned that secular people including aristocrats shall behave properly. After the instructions, these officials of the municipal

狂叫着通报他们的到来，斥骂左右两边的路人赶快避开，耀武扬威地骑马走一圈八廓（中环）之后，在大昭寺附近的一个角落下马安营扎寨，开始履行护卫拉萨二十一天的圣职。五世达赖喇嘛原是哲蚌寺的喇嘛，自然对该寺偏爱有加，他曾颁布特殊命令，任命哲蚌寺喇嘛们负责大祈愿法会期间拉萨社会治安。这个特殊的使命使哲蚌寺的喇嘛越发不可一世。他们开始执行这个使命时，要举行一场极有趣味的仪式。铁棒喇嘛一就职，就指定另外的两名代表，打扮得跟铁棒喇嘛一模一样，都拿着铁棒（权力的象征物），向大众宣布他们的权力。由魁梧高大、手持鞭棒的侍从作先导，这两名代表殿后来到拉萨市政府的门前。政府的大门紧闭，原来的门卫此前已经撤离，十二个市政府的职员站成四人一排，手里拿着帽子，在一堆冒烟的柴堆后面鞠躬，毕恭毕敬地聆听喇嘛们的指示。这两名代表轮流站出来，极其傲慢同时非常戏剧性地用洪亮的嗓音训话，提醒这些政府官员，在大祈愿法会期间维护拉萨的秩序是哲蚌寺喇嘛的独家权力，并告诫俗人包括贵族在内要举止规矩。听完训话，这些市政府的职员马上锁起办公室的门消失得无影无踪，直到大祈愿法会结束，权力才又重新回到他们手里。这两名代表还要去北部的一个山泉再做一番演说，敦促龙神在此重要时期保证供水。第三个讲演是一个流放令，专门发给城市寺庙的一名代表——色拉寺降神的嘎玛沙神灵。第四个训令在另一个泉水边宣布，如此这般，就结束了此番使命。"

拉萨每一年新年的大祈愿法会如今依然会举行，与达赖喇嘛时期相比，在如今的大祈愿法会上已看不到当时作为特权阶层的僧侣们那些趾高气扬的过场和仪式，更多的是喇嘛们诵经祈福，人们汇聚寺庙供奉而为来年许愿，再就是各种各样的

government locked the door of the office and disappeared, and the power returned to their hands after the completion of the Grand Prayer Ceremony. These two representatives came to a spring in the north and gave speeches and urged the Dragon God to guarantee floods in the important period. The third speech was an exile order which was issued to a representative of the urban temple especially, who was Gamatha God of the Salad Temple. The fourth instruction was declared beside another spring, then the mission ended in this way."

New Year Grand Prayer Ceremony is still held in Lhasa each year, and the previous arrogant formalities and ceremonies of the monks being the privileged class cannot be seen in present Grand Prayer Ceremony compared with that in the periods of Dalai Lama. Lamas chant and pray more often, people gather in the temples to pray for the coming year, and there are a variety of secular entertainment activities. Besides "Qiangmu" which is the traditional religious dance performance, there are more and more activities entertaining the mass in the late period, such as birthday star dance, wrestling, fighting and horse racing etc., which are activities entertaining gods as well as people. It's said that these secular activities are related to ancient people's influence on Tibet, which can be seen from the Mongolianization of activity forms including costumes and etiquette. On the fifteenth day of the first month during the Grand Prayer Ceremony, there is Ghee Lantern Festival, which has been the grandest activity for Lhasa to celebrate Tibetan New Year for years, which is similar to Chinese Lantern Festival. On this night, Eight Barkhor Street is filled with various kinds of flowers, patterns, figures, birds and beasts etc. which are made of five-colored ghee. Monks in the temples and folk artisans make all kinds of wonderful and colorful ghee flower disks and figures with different gestures, myth and legend stories and so on. Urban and town people crowd in Eight Barkhor Street to appreciate them and the revelry goes on all the night. Ghee Lantern Festival on the fifteenth day of the first month is one of the grandest parts of Tibetan New Year in Tibet, I will describe Ghee Lantern Festival especially in the latter chapter in detail.

世俗化的娱乐活动，除了传统的宗教舞蹈表演——"羌姆"，到后期越来越多的是穿插各种娱乐群众的活动，比如跳寿星舞、摔跤、角斗、赛马等，既是娱神也是自娱的活动。据说这些世俗化的活动跟蒙古人对西藏的影响不无关系，从活动的形式包括服装和礼仪上的蒙古化可以看出来。在大祈愿法会期间的正月十五那一天会有一个酥油灯会，这是拉萨庆贺藏历年最隆重的活动，类似于汉族的元宵节灯会。这一天晚上，八廓街四周会摆满五彩酥油塑成的各种花卉、图案和人物、鸟兽等，各寺僧人和民间艺人制作出各种精美多彩的酥油花盘和各种姿态的人物、神话传说故事等，城乡人民都纷纷涌到八廓街观赏礼拜，彻夜狂欢。正月十五酥油灯会是藏区藏历年最为隆重的一个环节之一，还有很多有趣的活动和传说故事，笔者将在之后的章节中用专门的篇幅再细致讲述酥油灯会的情况。

除了酥油灯会，在旧时西藏的新年期间，拉萨各寺院的僧侣还有一项最重要的仪式即新年的驱鬼仪式。驱鬼仪式是指在新年期间，下至百姓各家各户，上至各大寺庙和布达拉宫都一定会进行的仪式，意在祛除邪恶，祈福来年。如今在西藏的平常百姓家过新年还可以看到各家在屋内进行的驱鬼仪式，通常会在藏历年二十九那天进行，笔者在下个章节讲藏历年的习俗时还会具体讲到。而在旧时西藏，布达拉宫有专门的驱鬼法会，但今天这些寺庙内的驱鬼仪式大概还没有恢复过来，所以不太能见得到，但从文献上也可以看到一些记载：

往年，布达拉宫郎杰扎仓僧人们的赶鬼驱邪法会最为有名，叫作"孜古朵"，意思是十二月二十九日布达拉宫抛掷朵玛、赶鬼驱邪的活动。这天下午，拉萨城的百姓和郊区的农人，都涌到布达拉宫上面的德央夏广场，看赶鬼驱邪表演。时

Besides Ghee Lantern Festival, there was another important ceremony for the monks of the temples in Lhasa during the period of New Year in old Tibet, which was Ghost Driving Ceremony. It was the ceremony which must be held by every household, great temple and the Potala Palace in Tibet during New Year, and meant eliminating evils and praying for the coming year. At present, Ghost Driving Ceremony can be seen in houses of Tibetan common people when they celebrate New Year, which is usually held on the twenty-ninth day of Tibetan New Year, and I will talk about the conventions of Tibetan New Year in the next chapter. The Potala Palace had special Ghost Driving Ceremony in old Tibet, but it doesn't recover in these temples now and cannot be seen. We can only see its records in literatures:

In the past years, Namgyal Dratsang of the Potala Palace were famous for Devil Driving and Evil Expelling Ceremony, which was called "Ziguduo", meaning activity of throwing Duoma, driving ghosts and expelling evils in the Potala Palace on the twenty-ninth of the twelfth month. On the afternoon of this day, common people in Lhasa city and peasant in the suburbs crowded to Deyangxia Square on the Potala Palace to see the performance of driving ghosts and expelling devils. When it was the time, Mantra Lamas of Namgyal Dratsang blew trombones and cornettes, played dozens of sheep-skin drums and declared the beginning of Devil Driving Ceremony. Firstly, the warriors of the Grand Prayer Ceremony in ancient garments ran to the centre of the stage. They wore peacock feather helmets, held broadswords, lances, shields in their hands, fought with each other, fired muskets, and the sounds of guns and fighting were earth-shaking, which created the mood for the devil expelling activity. Peasant dancers coming form Zhebulin Manor played the semi-gods and semi-devils, and played the dance for the gods. Next, monks of Namgyal Dratsang played the dance of guardian warriors, one senior monk appeared on the scene with six junior monks, and it was said that they were the representatives of the monks of Central Plains who came into Tibet during the Tubo period, as well as the donors of the ceremony; the second batch of people appearing on the scene were called "Azhala", who had high noses and deep eyes, wore colourful garments and masks mixed with red, blue, yellow and green, and it was said that there were the symbol of South Asian missionaries in the early period. Shortly, sixteen ghosts of the King of Hell came on the scene, and they were the messengers of Tangqing Qujie who was the King of Hell. Among sharp noises and clamours, four white skeleton ghosts rushed, jumped, cried, ran, and threw Zanba flour to the audience, and carried a thing called "Lingga" in the middle of the stage. Lingga was the embodiment of the devil and looked very ugly.

辰一到，郎杰扎仓的密咒喇嘛便吹起了长短法号，擂动几十面羊皮法鼓，宣告驱鬼仪式开始。首先，传召大法会的古装骑士们奔跑到舞场中心，他们头戴孔雀翎头盔，身穿铁片铠甲，手拿大刀、长矛、盾牌，互相砍杀，鸣放火枪，枪声、杀声惊天动地，为驱邪活动制造气氛。来自折布林庄园的农民舞师，扮演天龙八部神灵，跳起了诸神的舞蹈。接下来，郎杰扎仓的僧人们跳金刚之舞，首先出场的是一个大和尚带六个小和尚，据说他们是吐蕃时期进藏的中原和尚代表，又表示是法会的施主；第二场批出场的名叫"阿扎拉"，一个个高鼻深目，衣袍五彩斑斓，面具有红、蓝、黄、绿，据说他们是早期南亚传教士的象征。紧接着十六个阎王鬼卒出场，他们是阎王唐青曲杰的使者。在一片尖利的叫声和喧闹声中，四个白色的骷髅鬼呼啸而上，又蹦又跳，又喊又叫，一边奔跑，一边向观众扬撒

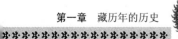

糌粑面，同时抬出一个名叫"灵噶"的东西，摆在舞场中心。灵噶是恶魔的化身，形象非常丑陋。这四个骷髅鬼名叫"多珠达巴"，意思是天葬场的守护神。接着，有一个白发苍苍、走路摇摇晃晃的老人出场，他用非常滑稽可笑的动作，打死了一个老虎模样的东西。据说，以前布达拉宫驱邪，并没有老人打虎的片段。20世纪初，十三世达赖喇嘛到五台山，看到了老人打虎的场面，回藏后让布达拉宫的僧人加进里面的。后面，二十四个黑帽咒师上场，他们拿起铁链，把恶魔化身的灵噶锁住，又用刀子、斧头和金刚杵砍杀灵噶，使他粉身碎骨。接着，驱邪活动最为惊心动魄的时刻来临了。一群喇嘛抬上一口大铁锅，里面装满菜子油，在油锅下面烧起大火，油锅沸腾翻滚，热浪冲向四方。黑帽咒师的首领，一手拿头盖骨颅器，里面装满高浓度的白酒，另一只手拿一张符咒，符咒上画着

These four skeleton ghosts were called "Duozhu Daba", meaning the patron saint of celestial burial site. Afterwards, an old man with white hair staggered on the stage, and he killed a thing which looked like a tiger with very funny actions. It was said that there was no plot of beating a tiger by an old man in ancient time. The thirteenth Dalai Lama came to Wutai Mountain in the early twentieth century. He saw the scene of an old man's beating a tiger, and let the monks in the Potala Palace added it after returning to Tibet. Later, twenty-four spellmakers with black hats appeared on the scene, they held the iron chain to lock Lingga which was the embodiment of the devil, and killed it into pieces with knives, axes and Vajras. Afterwards, the most thrilling moment of the devil expelling activity approached. A crowd of Lamas carried a huge iron pot, which was filled with rapeseed oil, burnt a big fire under the pot, which boiled and whose the hot surges were splashed in all directions. The leader of the spellmakers with black hats held a vessel which was filled with highly densed liquor in one hand, and a piece of spell on which the portrait of the devil was drawn. Suddenly, he poured the liquor into the oil pot, then there was a terrible noise, and the sky was filled with the blaze, and he throw the spell into the fire at the same time, the devil turned into dust and ashes in the blaze suddenly. The spellmakers rushed to invert the iron pot, chanted incantations and gestured, and marked a variety of fingerprints to suppress the devils, and this kind of spell was called "inverting pot", which meant that the devils were suppressed under the black iron castle, which cannot cause disorder and will never be reborn.

After inverting the pot, the monks carried the Duoma as high as a man and walked towards the base of the Potala Palace. Duoma was the embodiment of Tangqing Qujie, who was the King of Hell and had great deterrent power. The warriors put down the guns around it, cried and cleared the way, walked to the open field at the southern gate of the Potala Palace and put Duoma into the barley stack, which was burning in fury, and Duoma was burnt off, which symbolized that all ghosts had been expelled, and the Devil Driving Ceremony in the Potala Palace was completed.

Besides the Potala Palace, the home temples with living Buddhas, such as Mulu Temple, Danjielin Temple in South City, Cemolin Temple and Xidui Temple in North City, and Gongdelin Temple in West City all had the activities of throwing Duoma, driving devils and expelling evils on the afternoon

恶魔的图像。突然，他把白酒泼进油锅，油锅发出震耳欲聋的巨响，腾起冲天的火焰，同时把符咒抛进火中，恶魔顿时在火焰中化为灰烬。咒师们冲了上去，把铁锅倒扣，不停地念咒作法，打出各种镇压敌魔的手印，这种法术称为"扣锅"，意思是把恶魔们镇压在黑铁城堡下面，使它再也不能兴妖作怪，永世不得翻身。

扣锅之后，僧人们抬起一人高的朵玛，往布达拉宫下面走去，朵玛是阎王唐青曲杰的化身，有着很大的威慑力。武士们在它的周围放枪、吼叫、开道，一直走到布达拉宫南门外的广场，把朵玛放进青稞草堆，青稞草燃起熊熊的烈火，朵玛烧化了，表示所有的鬼物已经被驱走，布达拉宫的赶鬼仪式胜利结束。

过去，除布达拉宫以外，拉萨几座活佛的家庙、东城的木鹿寺、南城的丹杰林寺、北城的策墨林寺和锡堆寺、西城的功德林寺，这天下午都有抛掷朵玛赶鬼驱邪的活动。　　of this day in the past.

2. Tibetan New Year of Secular Official Class

Besides Dalai Lama, clerical and secular officials and aristocrats in old Tibet will hold a variety of ceremonies and celebrations in Tibetan New Year.

"The second day of the first month was the Tibetan King New Year. Before the seventh Dalai Lama, the Tibetan King system was carried out in Tibet. Dalai Lama was only the supreme religious leader, and administrative affairs were presided by a Tibetan King. Emperor Qianlong decided to eliminate the Tibetan King system, so that Dalai Lama was integrated with political and religious powers. Hereafter, Dalai Lama was the supreme religious leader as well as the supreme political leader in Tibet. On the celebration of the Tibetan King New Year, all clerical officials wore vphyar gru vpyastod costumes, all secular officials wore ancient costumes symbolizing rgal srid sna bdun, which was called 'rgya lu chas' meaning prince's costumes. According to the convention, two noble officials with Renjian costumes (treasury costumes) welcomed Dalai Lama to the throne in the West Chamber of Sunshine, and offered sacrifices such as eight auspicious things, seven religious treasures, eight holy things, delicious tea, crisp cake and so on. Treasury costumes were official garments made according to the memory of Awang Qizha, the local leader of Renbu Area in the period of the fifth Dalai

二、俗官阶层的藏历年

除了达赖喇嘛，在旧时的西藏还有噶厦政府各僧俗官员和贵族，他们在藏历新年的时候也会进行各自的仪式和庆典。

"正月初二是藏王新年。在七世达赖喇嘛以前，西藏实行藏王制。达赖喇嘛只是最高宗教首领，政务则由一位藏王主持。到乾隆皇帝时决心废除藏王制度，集政教两权于达赖喇嘛一身。从此，达赖喇嘛不但是西藏最高的宗教首领，又是最高的政治首领。在藏王新年的庆典上，所有的僧官都要穿恰珠恰堆服装，所有的俗官都要穿象征七政宝的古老服装，藏语叫'甲鲁切'，意思是王子装。在司西平措大殿里，照例有两位身着'仁坚装'（珍宝服）的贵族官员，把达赖喇嘛迎请到宝座上面，并进献八吉祥、七政宝、八圣物和香茶、酥糕等供奉。珍宝服是五世达赖喇嘛时期，根据仁布地方首领阿旺齐扎的回忆而制成的官服。届时，贵族官员要头戴缎帽，身穿缎袍，袍子上缀满了蜜蜡珠和松耳石。每年布达拉宫庆典，由贵族俗官轮流穿戴这种前朝的袍服，担任达赖喇嘛的典礼官和侍奉者，正典礼官由四品官出任，帽子是三角形的；副典礼官由五品官出任，帽子是圆形的。在庆典上，来自折布林庄园的农民舞师们，要表演象征天神、龙王、寻香、阿修罗、金翅鸟、夜叉、帝释、大腹行等天龙八部的神舞。八位舞童跳刀舞，十六位舞童跳尕巴舞。庆典最重要的一个内容，是达赖喇嘛接见新任命的官员，为他们摩顶祝福，藏话叫'三加'。受到达赖喇嘛的接见后，新官们便可以走马上任了。"

"正月初三还有一项欢庆活动，即以噶伦为首的各个品级的俗官，在布达拉宫北面的龙王潭园林里，举行盛大的新年宴会，欢庆佳节，然后转移到拉鲁草场，进行射箭比

Lama. Aristocrats and officials wore satin hats and satin gowns which were full of beeswax beads and pine otoliths (tophi) on occasions. Aristocrats and secular officials wore this kind of gowns of the previous dynasty in turn, and acted as ritual officials and attendants for Dalai Lama for the yearly Potala celebration, and rank four officials took up the post and wore cocked hats; rank five officials took up the post of adjutants and wore round hats. Peasant dancers from Zhebulin Manor performed the magic semi-god and semi-devil dance symbolizing heavenly god, dragon king, ghost, Asura, golden-wing bird, Yaksha, Sakka, Mahoraga and so on. Eight children played the knife dance, and sixteen children played the Gaba dance on the celebration. One of the most important contents of the celebration was that Dalai Lama met with newly-appointed officials, laid his hand on their heads and wished for them, which was called 'Sanjia' in Tibetan. After meeting with Dalai Lama, new officials can go to their posts."

"There was a celebration activity on the third day of the first month. Secular officials at all the ranks led by Galoins held the grand New Year party and celebrated the festival in the Dragon King Pool Garden in the north of the Potala Palace, and then they moved to Lalu Lawn to participate in an archery competition. They shot whistling arrows rather than ordinary arrows, many holes were carved on a piece of wood, which can whistle when they were shot. The archery competition was called 'Cisong Langda' meaning 'heavenly arrow on the third day'. Gaba performance team of the Potala Palace had performed for many times according to the convention. The song said that 'the places along the way have beautiful lotuses. High buildings and great yards of noblemen are superior to jeweled palaces in elfland's hills.'"

3. Tibetan New Year of Common People

The present way of Tibetan New Year celebrated by common people doesn't differ greatly from the previous way, the traditional convention has been passed basically and New Year celebration keeps a traditional procedure basically. From records of historical literature of people who visited Tibet, we can feel the scenes which Tibetans celebrated Tibetan New Year. The following paragraphs are taken from Evariste Régis Huc, the missionary of French Congregation, and records the scene that Lhasa people celebrated the Tibetans New Year in 1846 when he entered Tibet for exploration:

"As for Tibetan, year change was a chance to hold feast of celebration and happiness for all people. They prepared for New Year celebration on the last days of the twelfth month, and purchased

赛。他们射的箭不是一般的箭，而是响箭，在一根木头上面雕刻出许多洞，射出时发出呜呜的声音。这次射箭大赛，叫'次松朗达'，意思是'初三天箭'。布达拉宫的嘎巴演出队，照例要进行多场演出，歌词是：'沿途所说之地，莲花争妍斗奇。贵人高宅大院，胜过仙山琼阁。'"

三、普通百姓的藏历年

在普通百姓家里，藏历年的过法跟如今的相比变化不是那么大，传统的习俗基本都被传承下来，过年基本保持一个传统的程序。但也可以从过去进藏人士记载的历史文献当中，感受当时藏地人过藏历年的情形。下面一段是摘自法国遣使会士古伯察在1846年进入西藏探险时看到拉萨人过藏历年的情形：

"对于西藏人如同对于所有人一样，年代的更替都是一个举行盛宴庆祝和欢乐的时机，腊月的最后几天都用于准备过节，人们都购置了茶叶、酥油、糌粑、青稞酒和几块羊肉。他们从衣柜中取出最漂亮的衣服，掸去了平时都蒙于家具之上的灰尘。大家纷纷擦抹、扫除或清整。总而言之，人们都在设法使屋子更为整齐和干净一些。这种事仅仅每年出现一次，所有的家具都呈现出了一种新面貌，家中的祭坛特别受到了注意，把旧供像刷新，用新鲜酥油做成塔、花卉和用于装饰供养家佛的小佛堂等各种装饰物。"

"第一次祭祀仪式开始于子夜，因此所有的人都守夜，耐心地等待辞旧迎新的这一神秘而隆重的时刻。突然该城所有住宅区各个方向传来爆发的欢呼声。钟、锣、海螺、鼓和所有的西藏乐器声很快就交响成一片，产生了人们可以想象出的最为欢乐的场景。大家可能会说他们正在以一曲美妙的交响乐迎接新的一年的开始。"

"第二种仪礼是互相

tea, ghee, Zanba, barley wine and several pieces of mutton. They took the most beautiful clothes from wardrobe, and brushed off dust on furniture, and they wiped, cleaned or reorganized furnishings. All in all, people tried their best to make their houses tidier and cleaner. The thing only occurred once a year, all furniture had a new look, special attention was paid to altar at home, old Buddha images were brushed newly again, pagodas, flowers, and a variety of ornaments were offered to home Buddhas in small temples."

"The first sacrifice ceremony began at midnight, so all people stayed up late and waited for the mysterious and grand moment to ring out the old year and welcome the new one. Cheering sounds in all directions of all resident areas in the city came. Sounds of bells, gongs, conches and drums and all Tibetan music instruments were resounding, and became the scenes of joy. They may say that they were meeting with the beginning of New Year with the wonderful music."

"The second kind of etiquette was mutual

visiting, and new etiquette was adopted. When day was breaking, Tibetans ran to streets in the city. Ghee tea was held in one hand, and pyramid-shaped Zanbas were held in another hand with a broad golden painted plate on which three barley spikes on their top. In these days, visiting relatives and friends without Zanba and ghee tea wasn't allowed. Once they entered into the family which they hoped to visit, they knelt before the family altar thrice, decorated it ceremoniously and lighted the magic lamp. After some cedar leaves or other fragrant leaves (incense) were burnt in a big bronze incense burner, they offered a bowl of tea to the participant and gave a plate to them, and everyone took a handful of Zanba. The family members adopted the same etiquette to the visitors. Lhasa residents were accustomed to saying that Tibetan used Zanba and ghee tea to celebrate their New Year feast, while people of Central Plains used red-papered couplets and firecrackers, Kashmirians paid great attention to dishes and cigarette, and nomads celebrated festival with songs and dance."

"People can see some comedy troupes and street buskers in front of main public squares and buildings from morning till night, and performers

拜访，而且还是以新的仪礼进行。在天将破晓时，西藏人便奔向城市的街头，以一只手捧酥油茶，另一只手捧着装满捏成金字塔状的糌粑，并于其上部插三根青稞穗的镀金和着漆的宽大盘子。在这样的日子里，不允许不随身携带糌粑和酥油茶去访亲拜友。一旦进入希望向他们拜年的人的家庭时，便首先在家庭祭坛前跪拜三次，祭坛被隆重地装饰并点起了神灯。接着在一个大铜香炉钟焚烧了某些雪松或其他香树叶（煨桑）之后，便向出席的人献上一碗茶，向他们递上一个盘子，每个人都于其中取一撮糌粑。在家的人也向来访者作出同样的礼节。拉萨的居民都习惯说：藏人用糌粑和酥油茶来庆祝他们的新年盛宴，中原人则以红纸对联与爆竹，克什米尔人用讲究的菜肴和烟，游牧人用歌曲和舞蹈来庆祝节日。"

"在主要公共广场和公共建筑的前面，人们从早至晚都可以看到一些喜剧演员剧团和街头卖艺者，他们以其表演而使大众取乐。藏族人并不像中原人那样具有戏剧节目单，他们的喜剧演员们都同时和持续地出现在舞台上，有时唱，有时跳，有时又用力地和灵巧地旋转。舞蹈是这些人最为擅长的表演。他们旋转、跳跃，以一种确实令人惊奇的灵活性而单脚迅速旋转。这些人的服装是由一种上插雉鸡翎的直筒无边高帽、一种装饰以特长的白胡子的黑色脸谱、一条肥大的白裤子、一直垂到膝盖并由一条黄腰带紧扎于腰部的绿色长裙组成。在这件长袍上，每隔一段距离就有一条长绳，于绳子的一端悬挂很大的白羊毛团。当演员有节奏地摆动时，所有这些流苏都优雅地伴随着其身体的运动而摆动。当演员的身体开始旋转时，这些流苏便会横竖起来，于人身周围旋转，在某种意义上似乎是加入了其单足旋转。"

下面一段是藏学家沈宗濂、柳陞祺在1941

entertained the mass with their programs. Tibetans didn't have playbill like people of Central Plains, their comedians can appear on the stage at the same time continuously. Some of them sang, some of them jumped and they can rotate powerfully and flexibly. These people were skilled in dancing. They rotated, jumped and gyrated with one foot quickly with the surprising flexibility. Their costumes were made of toque with pheasant feather, black mask with very long beard, a pair of broad white trousers, and a green long skirt to knees with a yellow girdle which was firmly bounded on waist. There were a long rope on this gown in each gap and a large wool ball hang at one end of the rope. When actors swung rhythmically, all tassels swung gracefully with movement of body. When their bodies began to rotate, these tassels rotated around bodies and joined in their single-foot rotation."

The following paragraphs are some records of Shen Zonglian and Liu Shengqi about Lhasa's

Tibetan New Year in 1941:

"The new year celebration mood began to ferment in southern suburbs of Lhasa in the second half of the twelfth month. Men and women queued up for interview, and everyone waited for interview with a bundle of fuel and joined in chorus under the supervision of an official with a whip in his hand. Their fuel will be used for Grand New Year Prayer Ceremony. There will be over 20,000 Lamas getting together in Lhasa at that time. More people were busy in laying and repairing four flagpoles and hanging new prayer flags in Eight Barkhor Street, which was the main street. Households hung red and white cloth strips, prayer flags and sun-shielding cloth were newly polished. The year end approached, people cleaned house, new Thangka was changed in family hall receiving guests, piles of new fried ghee cakes and Qiema. There were a set of offerings to celebrate New Year: a bottle of liquor, an empty silver bowl, a wooden plate containing barley flour and a wooden plate containing wheat grains. Wheat straw, ghee stick and a red wild flower called 'New Year flower' were stuck upon wheat grains and barley flour."

年对拉萨过藏历年的一些记录：

"藏历十二月的下半旬，拉萨的南郊就开始酝酿过年的气氛了。前来应召的男男女女排成长队，在一名手持皮鞭的官员的监督下，每人带着一捆燃料，齐声唱着歌曲等待应聘。他们所带的燃料用于新年大祈愿法会。到时会有两万多喇嘛汇集在拉萨。更多的人在主要大街——八廓街上忙着放平四根旗杆，修修补补之后挂上新的经幡。家家户户都在窗上、门上挂起红色和白色的布条，房顶上的经幡和遮阳布都要焕然一新。年末将至，要大扫除，在接待客人的家庭经堂里换上新的唐卡，接着在每座祭坛前供上一堆堆新炸好的酥油糕和切玛。还有一整套过年的供品：一壶酒、一个空银碗、一个盛大麦粉的木盘和一个装小麦粒的木盘。在大麦粉和小麦粒上还插着麦秆、酥油棍和一种叫做'新年花'的红色野花。"

"除夕，人们用白粉在墙上、柱子上、房梁上和门前的空地上画上万字符、花瓶、花朵、太阳、月亮等这些表示吉祥的符号。全家人只吃一顿简单的晚饭，因为还有太多的事情要做。他们有个习俗，每个人都想在除夕夜第一个进入大昭寺，所以有一大群人在大昭寺门口守夜。午夜，沉重的大门刚开启一条缝，人群便蜂拥着冲向每一个殿堂，那儿的佛像已被装饰一新并点亮了酥油灯。这天晚上会有戴面具的人通宵达旦、逐门挨户地唱喜歌，祝家家来年喜庆满门。每家回报以哈达、酒、酥油糕和钱。除夕夜将尽，路上响起奔跑的马蹄声，这是政府官员穿着他们的新年盛装匆匆赶往布达拉参加早朝。"

总体来说，虽然藏历年随着时间的推移，期间不断加入各种新的元素，一些传统的宗教仪式和习俗也在时间的流逝中因为各种原因而消逝。但平常老百姓家依然保留着一

"On New Year's Eve, people used white powder to draw these lucky symbols such as Swastika, vase, flowers, the sun and the moon etc. on walls, poles, beams and clearings in front of doors. All family members only had a simple dinner, because there were too many things to do. They had a convention, which was that everyone wanted to enter the Jokhang Temple, so the crowds stayed at night at the gate of the Jokhang Temple. At midnight, the crowds charged into each hall when the heavy gate was opened, which had been decorated, and ghee lamps were lighted. People wearing masks sang blessing songs and sent best wishes for the coming year to each household all night long on that evening. Each family returned Hada, liquor, ghee cakes and money. When New Year Eve was completed, running horses' hooves rattled on the way, and goverment officials wearing their rich attires rushed to participate in pilgrimage in Potala."

Generally speaking, various kinds of new elements are added into Tibetan New Year as time goes on, while some traditional religious ceremonies and conventions disappear for different kinds of reasons. However, common people still keep a set of conventions to celebrate New Year with Tibetan

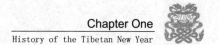

characteristics, and I will focus on how Tibetan common people celebrate Tibetan New Year by taking Lhasa area as an example in the next chapter.

套很有藏族特色的过年习俗，在下个章节笔者将以拉萨地区为例，重点介绍现在藏区平常老百姓家是如何过藏历年的。

第二章

藏历年的习俗

　　到了大年初一这天，按照习俗，这一天家里的主妇要起来得早早的。五点钟左右就要熬制一锅"观颠"，即是一种放有糟巴、红糖和奶渣的青稞酒，要给家里每人送上一碗。家人还没有起床，就要送到每人的被窝前，叫他们喝"观颠"，然后继续睡觉。主妇则要等到日出东方晨曦初露的时候，匆匆背上水桶去河边或者水井汲取新年的第一桶水，藏人视这桶水为圣洁、清甜的吉祥水，打到了这桶水在新的一年里就能免去许多灾难。天亮的时候，家里的人陆续起来了，全家人穿上新衣，洗漱完毕，按老少辈分坐下，长辈端来五谷斗，每人都先抓上几粒，向上方撒去，表示祭神，接着依次抓一点送进自己的嘴里。晚辈便开始向长辈恭贺新年，互道"扎西德勒"（吉祥如意）。

Chapter Two

Conventions of Tibetan New Year

On the first day of the first month, housewives get up early according to the convention. They make a pot of "Guandian", which is a kind of barley wine with dregs, brown sugar and milk residues, and present a bowl to each family member. If family members don't get up, they send "Guandian" to the bed of each family member, ask him or her to drink it, and then he or she keeps sleeping. Housewives wait till the sunrise and dawn, carry the first bucket of New Year water from the riverside or the well. Tibetans regard this bucket of water as holy, sweet and lucky water, and many disasters can be eliminated with it in New Year. At daybreak, family members get up consecutively, wear new clothes, sit down according to age and rank after washing and brushing. The senior members bring five-cereal bucket, and everyone grasps several grains and throws them upwards into the sky which symbolizes worshiping gods and grasps a few into his or her mouth to eat. The junior members begin to congratulate New Year to the senior members, and they say "Tashi Delek" (gook luck) mutually.

拉萨人过藏历年

Lhasa People's Celebration on Tibetan New Year

1. Preparation for New Year Celebration

Tibetans celebrate Tibetan New Year, and they are very busy in preparing for New Year celebration in the beginning of the twelfth month. Many things are prepared before New Year. Firstly, households begin to soak barley seeds, and people need to grow barley and wheat seedlings in basins and plates through delicate cultivation for several days. Barley seedlings will grow to one or two *cun* and be placed on niche table, which symbolize harvest and luck in the coming year.

Households begin to prepare for New Year foods and offerings since the middle of the twelfth month, which is the great event in New Year preparation works. Usually, housewives prepare for ghee and

一、过年前的准备

藏族人过藏历年，通常是一进入藏历的十二月便开始为新年的准备工作而忙得不可开交了。在新年之前有很多东西需要准备。首先，家家户户开始浸泡青稞种子，人们需要在盆盘里培育青稞苗和麦苗，经过若干天的精心栽培，藏历初一那天，要将长到一两寸的青稞幼苗，摆于佛龛茶几上，预祝新的一年丰收吉祥。

从十二月中旬开始，家家户户开始准备新年的食品和供品，这是新年准备工作当中的大事。通常都是一家的主妇们准备酥油和白面，另外是陆续炸"卡塞"（各种油炸的糕点和果子），"卡塞"的种类很多，有耳朵状的"苦过"，有长方形的"那夏"，有勺子形的"宾多"，有圆盆状的"布鲁"，还有大麻花状的"木冻"。这些卡塞需要累叠成"碟嘎"，"碟嘎"就是由这些不同形状的卡塞横一排竖一排垒放起来的供品，要供在正屋的佛龛前。通常是最下面几层放耳朵状的"苦过"，其上是长方形的"那夏"和大麻花状的"木冻"，再上面放圆盆状的"布鲁"，顶层是勺子状的"宾多"。然后再在"碟嘎"的上面摆放糖果、桃干、杏干、葡萄干、奶渣等食品①。过去，像这些"卡塞"都是要每家的主妇亲自准备的，如今因为藏区商业贸易的发达，和汉族一样，每年过年之前，

white flour, and fry "Kasai" in succession (a variety of fried cakes and pastes). There are diversified "Kasai", including ear-shaped "Kuguo", rectangular "Naxia", spoon-shaped "Bingduo", basin-shaped "Bulu", and braided "Mudong". These kinds of Kasai shall be stacked into "Diega", which is the offering stacked by "Kasai" in different shapes and will be sacrificed to the niche in the main building. Usually, several layers of ear-shaped "Kuguo" at the bottom with rectangular "Naxia" and braided "Mudong" placed on them, then basin-shaped "Bulu" is stacked on them, and spooned "Bingduo" is laid on the top. The foods such as candies, dried peaches and apricots, raisins, milk residues etc. are placed on "Diega"[①]. In the past, these kinds of "Kasai" were prepared by housewives themselves. Tibetan areas have developed commercial trades at present, so large cities in Tibet open trade markets selling goods specially before New Year like Han people, and shopping in New Year goods markets is the necessary event before New Year; as for Tibetans today, any goods which will be used for New Year celebration can be bought in markets; as for Tibetan sellers, they especially look forward to earning money to celebrate New Year in markets. Therefore, it took a lot of time to make things like "Kasai" in the past, while there are shops which especially fry a variety of "Kasai" in Lhasa, and buying them in shops directly can save a lot of time. However, some

①参见陈立明、曹晓燕著，《西藏民俗文化》292页，中国藏学出版社2003年版。

①Refer to Chen Liming and Cao Xiaoyan, *Tibetan Folk Culture*, p.292, China Tibetology Publishing House, 2003.

people insist on making foods by themselves. Every household must prepare sheep head which is a very important thing. Some sheep heads are real, and some are often made of ghee flour by some families, which are offered on tables before niches and called "Luguo". Sheep head is a mascot and symbolizes gook luck at the beginning of a year. A proverb says that "Tibetans place sheep heads, Han people set off firecrackers", which shows that Tibetans attach importance to sheep heads. Every household prepares a colorful five-cereal bucket, which is called "Qiema", which mainly symbolizes good harvest in the past year and wishes for good weather for the crops and bumper harvest. The five-cereal bucket is divided into two parts, one part is full of wheat grains and broad beans, another part is full of Zanba, on which barley spikes and Celosia stuck. The sun and moon plates are made of ghee flowers, and the five-cereal bucket has many auspicious patterns. These offerings need to be sacrificed on the offering table in front of the niche in the main building before the first day. "Dieka" is usually placed in the centre of the offering table, while other offerings are placed on its sides. Other delicious food can be placed as the offerings, and eight foods are placed in order to wish for good luck.

西藏各大城市都会开办专门置办年货的贸易市场，逛年货市场也几乎成了如今的藏人在过年之前必做的一件事，因为对今日的藏人来说过年要用到的任何年货都可以在年货市场上买到，对卖方的藏人来说他们也特别期盼在年货市场能够赚到一笔过年用的钱。所以，像"卡塞"这样的东西，过去要花很多时间来制作，现在在拉萨可以找到专门炸制各种"卡塞"的店，过年之前直接到店铺里去买可以省却不少时间。不过，依然还是有人会坚持自己做。另外还有一样非常重要的东西，也是每家每户都必会准备的，那就是羊头，羊头有些是真的，有些家会用酥油面粉制作一个，也供于佛龛前的供桌上，名叫"鲁过"。羊头是吉祥物，表示一年开头交好运的意思。有一句谚语叫："藏人摆羊头，汉人放鞭炮。"可见藏人对羊头的重视。每家每户还要准备一个彩色的五谷斗，名叫"切玛"，"切玛"

主要标志过去一年来的好收成，预祝新的一年风调雨顺，五谷丰盈。五谷斗一分为二，一边装满麦粒和蚕豆，另一边装满糌粑，上面插上鸡冠花、青稞穗，酥油花贴成日月牌，五谷斗周围绘满吉祥图案。这些供品都需要在初一之前供于正屋佛龛前的供桌上，一般是将"碟嘎"放在供桌的中心，其他供品以此为中心向两边排列，另外家里若有什么美味食品都可作为供品摆上一份，一般是摆八份以求吉祥。

在这期间，主妇们一般还要酿制青稞酒，准备酥油和牛羊肉。青稞酒在藏人的节庆日上的消耗量非常大，饮酒成了他们在节日上与人交流和娱乐最有效的方式，有人甚至通宵达旦地饮酒，狂欢至天亮。所以在节日之前每家每户酿制青稞酒也是个不轻松的活。

酿造青稞酒是一个系统的工程，从选料、浸

During this period, housewives make barley wine and prepare ghee, beef and mutton. Barley wine is consumed largely to celebrate Tibetan festivals, drinking wine becomes the most efficient way for them to communicate with and entertain people, and some people even drink wine all night and rejoice with wild excitement till dawn. Therefore, it's an uneasy thing for each household to make barley wine.

Making barley wine is a systematic project, and particular attention shall be paid to the processes from material selection, soaking, stewing and fermentation to blending, so not everyone can brew delicious barley wine. Tibetans in the cities drink barley wine, as well as various brands of beer and liquor on New Year's Day or other festivals at present. However, Tibetans in agricultural and pastoral areas like drinking their own barley wine, which can represent Tibetan characteristics in the best way. Barley wine of Shigatse is well-known all over Tibet, it's said that every household can brew wine, and there may be two hundred households living on selling wine.

Before New Year, men in villages will ride horses to "Holy Mountain" to cut fragrant cypress branches and bring them home, fragrant cypress branches are the main materials of "Weisang" which are sacrificed to gods everyday during New Year.

On the twenty-eighth or twenty-ninth day of the twelfth month, people begin to clean and decorate houses. Houses, rooms, passways of villages, even field ridges and corners are cleaned on lucky days, such as the third, fifth, seventh and ninth etc. days. Moreover, some families draw eight auspicious patterns including delicate lotus, precious umbrella, conch, dharma-cakra, aquarius, victory banner, golden fish and lucky tie on walls with white powder; scorpion symbolizing Dragon God, the sun,

泡、蒸煮、发酵到勾兑，每一个程序都很讲究，一点都不能马虎，因此也不是每个人都能够酿出好喝的青稞酒。现在在城市里面的藏人逢年过节除了饮青稞酒也买各种牌子的啤酒、白酒来喝。但是一般农牧地区的藏人还是喜欢自己酿青稞酒喝，也只有青稞酒才最能代表藏族的特色。在整个藏区，日喀则的青稞酒最有名，在日喀则据说家家户户都会酿酒，专门靠卖酒为生的大概就有两百户。

新年之前，各村寨男子还要骑马到附近的"圣山"去砍来柏香树枝，驮回家，这是过年期间每天向神灵"煨桑"的主要原料。

到了十二月二十八或二十九日这天，人们便开始打扫、装扮房屋。住宅上下、房屋里外、村寨走道，甚至田坎地角都要打扫得干干净净，而且打扫也要择吉日，比如3、5、7、9等。另外有些家还要用白粉在墙上画出妙莲、宝伞、海螺、法轮、宝瓶、胜幢、金鱼、吉祥结等八吉祥图案；厨房墙壁上画出象征龙神的蝎子，还有日、月、麦穗、炉灶、奶桶以及表示吉祥永固的雍仲图。屋内要换上新的彩色窗帘、门帘，换上新的卡垫，新的桌布等。除此之外，家里男女老少都要换新衣服，老少男子都要剃头，女子要洗梳发辫。总之就是屋子里里外外，从物到人都要给人焕然一新的感觉。

the moon, wheat spike, cooking range, milk barrel and Yongzhong pattern meaning luck and eternity are drawn on kitchen walls. New colorful window and door curtains, new cushions and table cloths shall be changed in houses. Moreover, all family members wear new garments, all men have haircuts and women wash and do their hair in braids. All in all, things and people in houses look completely new.

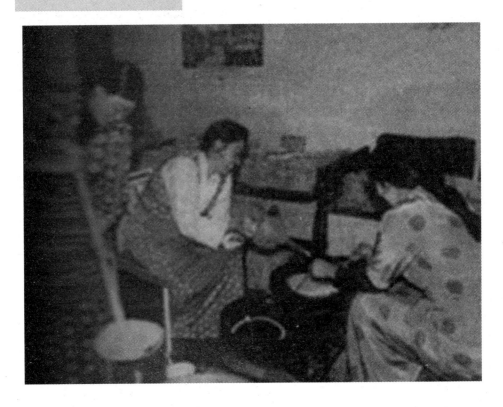

2. New Year's Eve, Eating "Gutu" and Ghost Driving

Eating "Gutu"

As for Tibetans, they often regard the twenty-ninth day of the twelfth month as New Year's Eve, which differs from Han people who regard the thirtieth day of the twelfth month as New Year's Eve. Because "nine" is a lucky number in Tibet, so the twenty-ninth day of the twelfth month is a lucky day. People bathe and wear new or clean clothes, wipe bodies with Zanba. Dirty wiped things and hair and nails which are cut off are put together, which will be sent away when ghosts are driven. "Gutu" is made next, which is a kind of dough ball eaten on the twenty-ninth day of the twelfth month, and is named after date since "Gu" represents twenty-nine and "Tu" means floury soup. Nine kinds of auspicious things will be put in "Gutu", mainly including mutton, Zanba, ginseng fruit, barley corn, round radish, milk residue, peach kernel, turnip and pea. Dough ball often has two forms, one kind is known as cat ear which is fingernail-sized, the other kind is larger and walnut-sized, and various kinds of things are put into it, including wool, white stone, pepper, charcoal, coin and so on; some of them will be made into the shapes such as the sun, the moon, "figures" with small head and big belly and so on.

二、除夕夜，吃"古吐"，赶鬼

吃"古吐"

对藏人来说他们通常习惯把腊月二十九这天视为除夕，和汉族视腊月三十为除夕不太一样。因为"九"在西藏是个吉祥的数字，所以腊月二十九是个吉祥的日子。到这一天人们除了要沐浴更衣，用糌粑擦拭身体，还要把擦下来的脏东西和剪下的头发指甲等集中放在一起，准备晚上赶鬼的时候一起送走。接下来，就要做"古吐"，"古吐"就是腊月二十九吃的一种面疙瘩，"古吐"是按照日期命名的，"古"即"九"表示二十九，"吐"是面糊羹的意思。"古吐"里面要放九种吉祥物，主要是羊肉、糌粑、人参果、麦粒、圆根、奶渣、桃仁、萝卜、豌豆等。面疙瘩通常会有两种形态：一种是指头大小的，俗称猫耳朵；另外一种比较大，有核桃那么大，里面包进各种各样的东西，如羊毛、白石子、辣椒、木炭、硬币等；有一些还会做成太阳、月亮、小脑袋大肚子的人等形状。

傍晚，一家男女老少便围坐在一起吃一顿例行的"古吐"，就相当于汉族年三十的团圆饭。吃"古吐"的时候，有人就会吃到包有各种各样东西的面疙瘩，这通常会惹得全家人哄堂大笑，因为每一样东西都有它的寓意。譬如，吃出羊毛，说明他（她）心地善良；吃出辣椒说明他（她）性格泼辣；吃出木炭，说明他（她）心黑；吃出石头，表示他（她）心肠很硬；吃出硬币，就表示此人会财运亨通；如果吃到大肚子娃娃的人，就要受罚，叫他（她）装狗叫、驴叫，还要喝九勺子面汤，通常每个人要吃三碗"古吐"。全家人就在那些"占卜"当中嬉笑怒骂，一家人其乐融融，每家每户洋溢着欢声笑语，快快乐乐地迎接新年的到来。

All family members sit around and eat a regular "Gutu" in the evening, which is similar to family reunion dinner on the thirtieth day of Han people. When eating "Gutu", some people will eat a variety of dough balls, and all of them burst into laughter, because each thing has its implied meaning. For example, eating wool symbolizes that he or she is kind-hearted; eating pepper symbolizes that he or she is straightforward; eating charcoal symbolizes that he or she is bad-hearted; eating stone symbolizes that he or she is hard-hearted; eating coin symbolizes that he or she will become wealthy; eating figures with big belly will be punished, he or she must pretend to cry like a dog or donkey and eat nine spoons of floury soap. Everyone eats three bowls of "Gutu" usually. All family members laugh and snarl among those "divinations". Everyone is pleasant, and each household is full of cheerful chatting and laughing and welcomes the coming of New Year happily.

Ghost Driving on New Year's Eve

After they are full, they undertake the next important event, i.e. "ghost driving", which is called "Lvzangba" in Tibetan. In the opinion of Tibetans, all kinds of ghosts exist in the world besides people and gods, which will bring diseases, disasters and disputes to people. Therefore, these ghosts around people must be driven out from houses and cities to places which cannot be seen and heard. This is one of the most important events in the conventions for Tibetans to celebrate New Year.

In the past, Ghost Driving Ceremony was held all over Tibet, it was held by different sects of religious temples, and the convention had influenced massive Tibetans deeply. I have introduced the Ghost Driving Ceremony in the Potala Palace in the old times especially in the former chapter. At present, the Ghost Driving Ceremony of big temples isn't complex, and it has been simplified and weakened in many aspects, but two processes must be undertaken. Before the day of driving ghosts, temples must make an enormous conical Zanba pagoda, which is called "Duoma" in Tibetan represents food being sacrificed to ghosts. Monks in temples will chant mantras for three days, seven days or longer time in front of Duomas in order to

除夕赶鬼

酒足饭饱之后，便要进入下一个很重要的环节，就是"赶鬼"，藏语叫做"吕藏巴"。在藏人的观念里，世界上除了人、神之外，还有各种各样的鬼环绕在四周，给人带来疾病、灾难和纠纷。所以，在新年来临之际，一定要把这些身边的鬼通通赶出家门，赶出城市，最终赶到眼睛看不到，耳朵听不到的地方去。这在藏人过新年的习俗中是最为重要的环节之一。

在旧时西藏，这一天，从上至下，包括各派宗教寺庙都会进行赶鬼仪式，这个习俗在广大藏族人心中有着根深蒂固的影响。在上个章节当中，笔者已经用专门的篇幅介绍了旧时布达拉宫的驱鬼仪式。如今各大寺院的驱鬼仪式已经没有那么繁复，在很多方面都简化和淡化，但主要还有两项要进行。一个是在驱鬼这天以前，寺庙就必须制作巨大的圆锥形糌粑塔，藏语叫

045

做"朵玛"，这代表施舍给鬼的食物。寺院僧人们要对着"朵玛"念三天、七天甚至更长时间的密咒，以便使护法神的威力注入这些"朵玛"当中，鬼吃了这些"朵玛"就会被赶走、降伏。僧人念经咒是非常辛苦的事情，常常从天明念到天黑，从天黑再念到天明，一时一刻都不能离开，吃东西、上厕所时也要找人替代。一个"朵玛"就象征一个护法神，或者是护法神的化身，"朵玛"的颜色通常会不一样，形状也会不同。到了二十九日的傍晚，这些"朵玛"便被抛掷出去，或者用大火焚烧，称为"朵加"，意思是抛掷"朵玛"，据说妖魔们吃了这些"朵玛"，就被护法神灵所降伏或驱赶了。另外一项重要的活动是在二十九日这天的白天，各大寺院会在各自寺院前的广场上进行一些金刚舞的表演，即跳神，并进行驱魔送鬼仪式，不过仪式比旧时已经简化很多了，但是还是会吸引若干

put power of protective gods into them, and ghosts will be driven away and vanquished. It's uneasy for monks to chant mantras from morning till night, from night till dawn, they cannot leave and eat for a moment, and somebody will replace them even they go to toilet. A Duoma symbolizes a protective god or the embodiment of a protective god, and Duomas have different colors and forms usually. These Duomas will be thrown out or burnt by big fire on the evening of the twenty-ninth day, which is called "Duojia" meaning throwing Duomas. It's said that ghosts are vanquished or driven away by protective gods after eating these Duomas. Another important event is that some dharma dances are performed in the daytime on the twenty-ninth day on squares of big temples, i.e. dancing to gods, and the ceremony of driving ghosts is undertaken, but it is simpler than that in the old times, and will attract many common people to watch, and a variety of entertainment activities will be performed after these dances usually.

老百姓前来观看，现在通常在这些跳神舞之后还会加上各种娱乐活动。

However, folk ghost driving ceremony is often undertaken in the evening. After eating "Gutu", people pile up several stone stacks in their courts which symbolize thrones of ghosts, and several broken ceramic pots symbolizing ghosts' "rice bowls" are placed in front of the thrones, and then people pour the rest of "Gutu" and things wiped from their bodies with Zanba into ceramic pots in the daytime, which symbolize abominable odors. They ask ghosts to have the rest of "Gutu" as dinner, and masters persuade them continuously, "Please have a big meal!" As soon as the moment comes, masters kick over the thrones of ghosts, fire torches and cry in every room, "Ghosts, come out! Ghosts, come out!" At last, some people carry the broken ceramic pots, some people hold the torches high, and cry the slogan of ghost driving loudly, "Ghosts, get out of here! Ghosts, get out of here!" Some people drive ghosts to the pool beside the square, some people drive ghosts to the side of Lhasa River, break the ceramic pots into pieces and fire barley stacks, and the big fire proves that ghosts run away and are burnt, and they sing songs, cheer and come home happily. Therefore, streets and lanes are ablaze with lights in Lhasa in the evening on the twenty-ninth day of the twelfth month, and people's yells of driving ghosts are heard everywhere lively. People divide cleaned garbage into nine piles in Maizhokunggar villages near Lhasa, and pile them

而民间的驱鬼仪式一般都是在晚上进行。在吃过"古吐"之后，人们在自家的庭院内垒几个石堆，代表鬼的宝座，在宝座的前面，摆几个破陶盆，代表鬼的"饭碗"，然后人们往陶盆里面倒吃剩下的"古吐"，还有白天从每个人身上用糌粑团擦下来的东西，代表人的秽气和疾病之类的。先请鬼用餐，吃这些剩下的"古吐"，主人还要一直不停地在旁边劝说："吃吧，吃吧，吃得饱饱的吧！"时间一到，主人便一脚踢翻了鬼的宝座，点起火把，到每一间屋里吼："鬼，出来！鬼，出来！"最后，有些人端着破陶罐，有些人高举着火把，同声高呼赶鬼的口号："鬼，滚蛋吧！鬼，滚蛋吧！"有的把鬼赶到广场水坑边，有的把鬼赶到拉萨河畔，在那里把破陶罐砸碎，点燃青稞草堆，熊熊大火证明把鬼烧跑了、烧化了，然后唱着歌、欢呼着，高高兴兴地回家。所以，在腊月二十九的晚上，拉萨各街巷灯火通明，到处听得到人们赶鬼的吆喝声，热闹非凡。拉萨附近的墨竹工卡农村，人们把清理出来的垃圾分成九堆，堆在十字路口，各家各户赶鬼的人，通通在十字路口汇集，中间用青稞草燃起篝火，所有人围着篝火跳果谐，唱藏戏，欢庆赶鬼的胜利。回家的时候，家里人还会在院子里烧起一堆火，回来的人必须一个接着一个从火堆上跳过去，以此证明他们并没有把鬼物或者灾难带回来，赶鬼活动才算圆满结束。

at the crossroads. People driving ghosts from each household get together at the crossroads, with a bonfire burnt with barley grass. All of them dance Guoxie, sing Tibetan opera, and celebrate victory of driving ghosts. The family members burn a pile of fire at yard, and people coming back must jump over the fire pile one by one when they come home in order to prove that they don't bring ghosts or disasters home, and the ghost driving activity ends completely.

3. Family Union and Worshiping Buddhas on the First Day of the First Month

On the first day of the first month, housewives get up early according to the convention. They make a pot of "Guandian", which is a kind of barley wine with dregs, brown sugar and milk residues, and present a bowl to each family member. If family members don't get up, they send "Guandian" to the bed of each family member, ask him or her to drink it, and then he or she keeps sleeping. Housewives wait till the sunrise and dawn, carry the first bucket of New Year water from the riverside or the well. Tibetans regard this bucket of water as holy, sweet and lucky water, and many disasters can be eliminated with it in New Year. At daybreak, family members get up consecutively, wear new clothes, sit down according to age and rank after washing and brushing. The senior members bring five-cereal bucket, and everyone grasps several grains and throws them upwards into the sky which symbolizes worshiping gods and grasps a few into his or her mouth to eat. The junior members begin to congratulate New Year to the senior members, and they say "Tashi Delek" (gook luck) mutually. Afterwards, they begin to have breakfast including porridge and ginseng fruits, and toast barley wine mutually. In some pastoral regions, housewives boil sheep heads according to number of family members, and carry them on a plate in front of the oldest man, who distributes a sheep head and a knife to everyone according to age in turn. People

三、初一家庭聚会，朝佛

到了大年初一这天，按照习俗，这一天家里的主妇要起来得早早的。五点钟左右就要熬制一锅"观颠"，即是一种放有糟巴、红糖和奶渣的青稞酒，要给家里每人送上一碗。家人还没有起床，就要送到每人的被窝前，叫他们喝"观颠"，然后继续睡觉。主妇则要等到日出东方晨曦初露的时候，匆匆背上水桶去河边或者水井汲取新年的第一桶水，藏人视这桶水为圣洁、清甜的吉祥水，打到了这桶水在新的一年里就能免去许多灾难。天亮的时候，家里的人陆续起来了，全家人穿上新衣，洗漱完毕，按老少辈分坐下，长辈端来五谷斗，每人都先抓上几粒，向上方撒去，表示祭神，接着依次抓一点送进自己的嘴里。晚辈便开始向长辈恭贺新年，互道"扎西德勒"（吉祥如意）。之后大家便开始一起吃早餐，一般是吃麦片粥和酥油拌的人参果，再互相敬青稞酒。在一些牧区，主妇还要按照家庭成员的数目煮好羊头，用食案捧到年龄最大的男子面前，由他依长幼的次序分发给每人一只羊头、一把小刀。大家围着火炉一面割羊头肉吃，一面互祝新年家庭和睦，人增畜旺。大年初一这一天，各家基本闭门欢聚，互相不走访，都在家里与家人进行娱乐活动或者佛事活动。

西藏居民普遍信仰藏传佛教，拉萨人也不例外。他们在新年的头一天一定要到寺庙敬神朝佛。拉萨人朝佛的地方，主要是大昭寺和小昭寺。人们准备好一个灯盏，灯盏里注满酥油。如果天气晴好，又无风，朝佛者便会把灯盏点亮，端着朝大昭寺和小昭寺走去。这时候，在曙光初现的拉萨古城，到处都能看到灯光闪闪烁烁，如同夜空中灿烂的群星。

在大昭寺，主要朝拜文成公主带来的佛祖释迦

sit around a stove, cut and eat mutton, and they wish family's harmony, increase of family members and growth of livestock. On the first day of the first month, every family close doors to get together happily, don't visit one another, stay at home with family members to participate in entertainment activities or Buddhism activities.

Residents in Tibet believe in Tibetan Buddhism usually, including Lhasa people. They must go to temple to worship gods and Buddhas on the first day of New Year. The places in which Lhasa people worship Buddhas are mainly the Jokhang Temple and the Ramoche Temple. People prepare a lamp which is full of ghee. If it is fine and there is no wind, the worshipers will light the lamp and walk towards the Jokhang Temple and the Ramoche Temple. When the day breaks in the ancient Lhasa city, lights can be seen everywhere like brilliant stars at night.

People worship gold statues including Shakyamuni Buddha in his twelve years old brought to Tibet by Princess Wencheng, the eleven-faced Avalokitesvara Tuoqi Qinbo with magic power, three famous Maitreya Buddha statues and the statue of Glorious Goddess as the protective god mainly in the Jokhang Temple. People worship the statue of Shakyamuni Buddha in his eight years old brought to Tibet by Nepal princess and Amitayus Buddha blessing people's health and longevity mainly in the Ramoche Temple.

Worshippers present Hadas to Buddhas at first, and then pour melted ghee of their own lamps to ever-burning lamps, which symbolizes that their hearts of piety and esteem to gods burn with their cores gradually. Afterwards, they donate affordable coins in charity boxes, then touch foreheads to knees and thrones of Buddhas tightly, and mutter their desires and hopes for New Year in a low voice at last. They often say in a low voice like chatting with gods and Buddhas.

4. Visiting Relatives and Friends and Paying New Year Calls on the Second Day of the First Month

On the second day, relatives and friends begin mutual visiting and treatment, which lasts for three to five days continuously. On this day, people will wear new clothes and the most beautiful ornaments

牟尼十二岁等身金像，具有神变的十一面观音托其钦波，还有三尊著名的弥勒强巴佛像，以及二楼的吉祥天女护法神像。在小昭寺，主要朝拜尼泊尔公主带来的佛祖释迦牟尼八岁等身像明久多吉、保佑人们健康长寿的无量寿佛等。

朝佛人先给神佛献上哈达，接着把自己灯盏里融化了的酥油注入佛像前的长明灯里，表示自己对佛的虔诚和崇敬之心正跟着长明灯的灯芯一起缓缓燃烧。然后往功德箱里，奉献自己力所能及的钱币，最后把额头紧紧贴在佛的膝盖和宝座上面，喃喃讲述自己新的一年的愿望和祈求。他们往往把声音放得很低很低，好像在和神佛交谈。

四、初二走亲访友，拜年

到了初二这天，亲朋好友便开始串门拜年，互相请客拜访，一般要持续三五天。到这天，人们都要穿新装、戴最漂亮的首饰，捧着"切玛"去拜年。即使经济条件再不好的人，也要准备一件过年的新袍子，或一两件比较粗糙的装饰品。在西藏的民间有个古老的说法，法王辛者曲杰每逢年节都要从铜镜里观察世人的生活，如果大家穿得漂漂亮亮、暖暖和和，他便十分高兴，会给世人新的恩惠；如果他看见众生穿得破破烂烂，便心灰意冷，甚至一怒之下，还会降下灾害和瘟疫使百姓陷于水深火热之中。因此，过年穿新衣有取悦神王赐福的意思。

来到亲戚朋友家拜年的人先在门外高声说："罗桑尔让（新年好）！扎西德勒（吉祥如意）！"主人听到后便捧着自家的"切玛"五谷斗出来到门口迎接，也向客人问候。客人用手捏取"切玛"里的一点糌粑、青稞向天空抛洒三次，供奉天神、虚空神和勒神；然后在嘴里尝一点，和主人互相敬献哈达，

to pay New Year calls with "Qiema". Even people whose economic conditions aren't well prepare new gowns for New Year and one or two pieces of coarse ornaments. There is an old folk saying in Tibet, Dharmaraja Xinzhe Qujie observes people's life through a bronze mirror on festival occasions, he will be pleased and bring new kindnesses to the world if he sees everyone wearing beautifully and warmly; he will become depressed and bring disasters and plagues to common people and let them suffer greatly in a fury if he sees all people are in rags. Therefore, people wear new clothes to celebrate New Year in order to please the holy king for blessings.

When people come to houses of relatives and friends to pay New Year calls, they shout loudly outside doors and say, "Happy Losar (Happy New Year)! Tashi Delek (Gook luck)!" When hearing the words, masters meet them at gates with their own "Qiema" five-cereal buckets and greet guests. Guests take a few of Zanba and barley and threw them to the sky thrice to sacrifice to the Heavenly God, the Void God and Le God, then taste a few, exchange Hadas and barley wine with masters mutually, dip and sprinkle wine with ring finger thrice before drinking wine to sacrifice to heavenly and earthly gods. This is the form for friends and neighbors to pay New Year calls; if relatives and good friends pay New Year calls, they usually go into houses, and guests say "Tashi Delek!" when they enter houses, and masters stand up immediately and answer, "Happy Losar (Happy New Year)!" Afterwards, they exchange Hadas mutually, and masters carry "Qiema" firstly after guests are seated, and ask them to sacrifice a handful to the heaven, earth and god respectively, and then take a handful to taste themselves. Masters carry Tibetan high-necked and long-mouthed wine pot to propose a toast, and guests drink up full bowl of wine in three sips. Masters will ask relatives and good friends to sing songs and propose a toast if guests cannot drink up or out of politeness till they become drunk pleasantly.

On this day, people bless, propose toasts, sing, dance and rejoice with excitement in streets of Lhasa. No matter if people know one another or not, they will not let you pass if you don't drink three bowls of wine. Lhasa becomes a city of happy songs and dance which is filled with wine fragrance, and people sing songs and dance in groups and enjoy heartily. Folk artists in Tibet perform everywhere on this day, families with good conditions will invite folk artists to perform songs, dances and operas at home. Some artists will take the initiative to drop

互相敬青稞酒，喝酒前同样要用无名指蘸酒弹洒三次，供奉天地诸神。这是一般朋友和邻居之间的拜年形式，如果是亲戚之间或者是特别好的朋友之间则一般要进门去拜年，入门时客人道一声："扎西德勒！"主人要立即起身回敬一句："罗桑尔让（新年好）。"然后互赠哈达，客人入座后，主人先端来"切玛"，请贵客敬奉天、地、神各一撮，再自己撮一撮品尝。然后主人提着藏式高颈长嘴酒壶敬酒，客人分三口喝光满碗，若喝不完或者是客套，主人便会委托亲戚好友唱歌来敬酒，一直到客人尽兴微醉才罢休。

拉萨这天的街上，到处都在祝福敬酒，歌舞狂欢。人们不管认不认识，不喝三碗不会放你通过，拉萨成了一个欢乐歌舞之城，漫溢酒香之城，人们成群结队，载歌载舞，尽情狂欢。在这一天，西藏的民间艺人也四处活动，一些家庭条件比较好的人家还会专门请民间艺人到家来歌舞演戏助兴，有些艺人会主动串门演戏，头戴白面具，手持木棍等，即兴编唱歌词来讨主人开心。在街头和村子里，人们还自发组织群众性的歌舞和藏戏演出，这些自娱性的演出活动要持续三五天。

五、初三挂幡祈福

到藏历的初三，要敬奉"屋脊神"。人们登上各家的屋顶，拔去旧的经幡，把崭新的经幡插在屋顶上，经幡通常是印着经文的五彩旗帜。然后煨燃柏枝，叫做"煨桑"，"煨"为汉语，是燃烧不见火焰的意思，"桑"是藏语，是冒烟的意思，所以有人将"煨桑"翻译成"烧烟烟"、"烧神烟"。插完经幡之后，再向空中抛洒糌粑，飘动的经幡和袅袅上升的"桑烟"寄托着人们新年的祈愿飘向远方。喝过早茶，拉萨的男男女女便成群结伴到山上挂经幡，通常是到东郊的宝瓶山和西

around and play acts in houses, and they wear white masks, hold wooden sticks in hands, make lyrics extemporaneously to please masters. People can organize common people to perform songs, dances, and Tibetan operas spontaneously, and these self-entertainment performance activities will maintain three or five days.

5. Hanging Prayer Flags and Praying on the Third Day of the First Month

On the third day in the Tibetan calendar, the Roof Ridge God shall be sacrificed. People climb on roofs of their houses, pull out old prayer flags, erect brand-new prayer flags on roofs, and prayer flags are colorful and printed with scripture. Afterwards, they fire cypress branches, which is called "Weisang",i. e. "Wei" is Chinese which means burning without flame, and "Sang" is Tibetan, which means smoking, so some people translate "Weisang" as "burning smoke" or "burning holy smoke". After erecting prayer flags, they throw Zanba to the sky. Flying prayer flags and rising smoke symbolizes people's New Year wishes drifting to afar. After drinking morning tea, Lhasa men and women hang prayer flags on hills in groups, they often go to Precious Bottle Mountain in the eastern suburbs and Medicine Mountain in the western suburbs. More people climb Precious Bottle Mountain which is regarded by local people as the residence of Zhizunzan God controlling climates of Lhasa

Valley, harvest and failure of crops. After passing Lhasa River Bridge, people climb the mountain till the summit, burn holly smoke and erect prayer flags. Prayer flags erected here differ from those erected on roofs of houses. There are animal zodiacs of erecters on prayer flags, which symbolize their fates, and it's said that the higher prayer flags are erected, better fate and luck they will have, and more successful life. After erecting prayer flags, people will come to Lhasa riverside, tie prayer flags on willow branches beside the river, as were both sides of chain bridges and roads. Colorful prayer flags will fly above different sizes of bridges shortly on this day. Tibetans believe in Buddhism, so they often chant various kinds of scriptures, and it's said that chanting ten thousand times can shorten a samsara. In order to chant more scriptures, they make pray wheels and these "wind-horse flags" like prayer flags, which are printed with six-character mantras, as well as scriptures and their animal zodiacs. They are erected at hilltop or riverside, and fly in hill wind like horses running forward, and one flying is equal to chanting scriptures once.

郊的药山，宝瓶山去的人更多，这座神山被当地人认为是掌管拉萨河谷阴晴雨雪、农牧丰歉的直尊赞大神的住地。过了拉萨河大桥，人们便不停地往山上爬，一直要爬到山顶，然后煨烧神烟，插上经幡。通常这里插的经幡和在家里屋顶上插的不太一样。这里的经幡上通常写着插幡者的生辰属相，代表着插幡人的命运，据说经幡插得越高，表示他的命运会越好，福气越大，生活越顺利。插完经幡之后，人们通常会来到拉萨河边，在河边的柳枝上系满经幡，也有系在铁索桥、公路桥两侧的。这一天，不久便会看到大小桥梁上面飘扬着五颜六色的经幡。藏人因笃信佛教，所以平常嘴里都不断念诵着各种经文，据说每念十万遍可缩短一次轮回。为了念更多的经，他们制作了转经筒，还有像经幡这些"风马旗帜"，上面通常印满六字真言，各种经文，还有自己的生辰属相，插在山头或者水边，山风吹拂，旗帜飞舞，就像马儿在奔腾前进一般，每飘动一次，就相当于念了一遍经文。

插完经幡后，通常邻居亲友等三三两两地找一处背风向阳的坡地在一起唱歌、喝酒、谈笑、玩游戏，通常是不醉不归。那一天在山上四处都听得到人们的欢声笑语。

After erecting prayer flags, neighbors, relatives and friends sing songs, drink wine, chat, laugh and play games on the leeward slopes in the sunny side, and return home till they are drunk. People's happy voices and laughter are heard all over hills on that day.

6. The Beginning of the Grand Prayer Ceremony on the Fourth Day

Till the fourth day, Lhasa holds the Grand Prayer Ceremony which is the most solemn ceremony. In old Tibet, common people celebrated Tibetan New Year till the third day, because iron-rod Lamas managing Prayer Ceremony forbade them to sing, dance, drink wine and revel during the Grand Prayer Ceremony starting from the fourth day. In the previous chapter, I have introduced the scenes of the Prayer Ceremony in Lhasa in old Tibet, which is one of the most important four Buddhist affairs of Gelug Sect of Tibetan Buddhism and has had the history of five hundred years till now since it was founded by Tsongkapa. At present, the Jokhang Temple still holds the Prayer Ceremony on the fourth day in Tibetan New Year and the ceremony lasts till the fifteenth day of the first month continuously each year. During the Prayer Ceremony, nearly twenty thousand monks from the three grand temples get together in the Jokhang Temple and pray to the statue of Sakyamuni Buddha, and join scripture debate and exams for Geshe degree. The government distributes offerings to monks, and followers of Tibetan Buddhism in Tibet and other places come here to acquire lamps, worship Buddhas and donate with liveliness.

六、初四传召大法会开始

到了初四，拉萨要举行每年最隆重的传召大法会。所以在旧时西藏，一般老百姓的藏历年就过到初三为止，因为通常从初四开始的传召大法会期间，管理法会的铁棒喇嘛会禁止老百姓唱歌跳舞，也不允许喝酒狂欢。在上个章节中，已经用专门篇幅介绍过旧时西藏拉萨的传召法会的情况，这个法会是藏传佛教格鲁派每年最重大的四大佛事之一，从宗喀吧创制至今已经有五百年的历史了。如今的大昭寺依然在每年藏历初四左右举行传召法会，一直持续到元月十五。法会期间，西藏三大寺的僧人近2万人集中在大昭寺，向释迦牟尼的佛像祈祷，并举行辩经、格西学位考试。除政府给僧众发放布施外，西藏及其他地方的藏传佛教信众也到此添灯供佛布施，热闹非凡。

七、初五启耕节

藏历正月初五，拉萨郊区的农民会举行隆重的启耕节，表示他们春耕大忙的日子就要来临了。这一天，人们穿上节日的盛装，耕牛的额头上贴着酥油图案，犄角上插着彩旗和彩色羽毛，牛轭上披挂着缀满贝壳和松石的彩缎，尾巴上系着五彩缤纷的绸带。开耕之前，农人还要从家里扛出一块白色山石，那是去年从农田请回收藏好的，重新恭恭敬敬安入农田中央，称为"阿妈色多"，意即"金石头妈妈"，是庄稼的保护女神。农人在地里煨起桑烟，插上祈福幡，赶着牛，围绕着白石耕出五条畦子。每畦撒一种作物，例如豌豆、青稞、小麦、油菜籽、蚕豆等。启耕礼完毕，大家会聚一处，一边喝酒，一边唱歌，随着酒碗的轮转，歌声弥漫在整个初春的河谷，直到太阳西沉，尽兴而归。

7. Tillage Starting Festival on the Fifth Day

On the fifth day of the first month in the Tibetan calendar, peasants in the suburbs of Lhasa hold the grand Tillage Starting Festival, which symbolizes the coming of busy tillage. On this day, people wear festival costumes, the ghee pattern is stuck on foreheads of farm cattle, colorful flags and feathers are inserted on their horns, colorful satins which are full of shells and turquoises on yokes, and colorful ribbons are tied on their tails. Before starting tillage, a peasant carries a piece of white rock from his house, which was carried from their farmland last year and collected in his house. The rock placed in the centre of the farmland respectfully again, which is called "Ama Seduo", which means "the mother of gold stone", and is the protective goddess of crops. Peasants burn smoke in field, erect prayer flags, drive cattle, plow five segments of land around the white stone. A kind of crop is thrown into each segment, for example, pea, barley, wheat, rapeseed and broad bean. After the completion of the Tillage Starting Festival, people will get together, drink wine and sing. The valley is filled with songs with rotation of wine bowls, they will return home pleasantly till the sunset.

8. Tibetan New Year in Temples

Tibet is a society which is deeply influenced by religion, and there are a lot of monks in temples besides common people. Monks in temples celebrate Tibetan New Year with stronger religious colors, which differ from common people. Let's take Ta'er Temple in Qinghai as an example and see how Tibetan monks celebrate Tibetan New Year.

Since the thirtieth day, "Zhuosuo Qiemas" are placed in temples, mansions of living Buddhas and houses of monks.

On the morning of the first day of the first month,

八、寺院里的藏历年

西藏是一个深受宗教影响的社会，除了一般的老百姓，在寺院里还有大量的僧侣。寺院里僧人们过藏历年自然是充满了更加浓重的宗教色彩，有别于一般老百姓。以青海的塔尔寺为例来一窥僧人过藏历年的情况。

从三十日开始，在寺院、活佛府邸及各僧人家中摆设制作好"卓索切玛"。

大年初一的清晨，

塔尔寺大拉让吉祥新宫殿顶吹奏吉祥右旋白法螺，活佛、僧伽起床洗漱后，烧酥油茶，首先沾一点向空中遍洒三下，敬献天地神佛，而后自己喝几口以示分享祥瑞，随后穿戴新袈裟僧帽去大经堂诵经礼佛。两位执事僧请措钦夏俄大僧官和大会引经师来主持礼佛的祈祷活动。僧众唪诵大威德金刚、护法神母、放生等经典后，全体祈祷者拜见大法台。与此同时，在大经堂顶层和三大学院中也诵经祈祷。祈祷新的一年里佛法增盛，人民安康，百病消散，五谷丰登。八位大小喇吉和各活佛府邸携带贺年礼品去拜见大法台，对三大堪布和襄佐只作新年祝贺而不送礼品。祈祷礼佛仪式结束以后，接着举行新年斋茶会，大僧官、总管、祭供师等人到吉祥新宫来请大法台赴斋茶会。大法台从僧众中间走到上首铺设的红毡上转身向僧众拱手作揖，祝贺新春佳节，然后坐在首席位上，三大堪布和

the white right-rotational conches are played at the top of the New Auspicious Larang Palace of Ta'er Temple. Living Buddhas and monks heat ghee tea after getting up, washing and brushing, they dip a few and sprinkle the tea thrice to the sky, worship heavenly and earthly gods and Buhhdas, then they drink a few sips of it to share auspiciousness, and wear new kasayas and monk hats to chant sutras and worship Buhhdas. Two hierodeacons invite the Grand Administrator of Cuoqin Xia'e and the master chanter of the ceremony to preside praying activity of worshiping Buhhdas. After monks chant the canons such as Yamantaka, Protective Goddess, Releasing Captured Animals and so on, and all prayers visit the Grand Master. Meanwhile, people chant sutras and pray at the top floor of the main assembly hall and the three institutes. They pray for prosperity of Buddhism, health and welfare of people, elimination of diseases and harvest of five cereals. Eight grand and small Lajis and all clerks of houses of living Buhhdas bring New Year presents to the Grand Master, and pay New Year visits to the three Grand Khenpos and supervisors without presents. After the completion of the ceremony of praying and worshipping Buhhdas, New Year vegetarian tea meeting is held. Grand monk officials, general directors and officiants etc. come to the New Auspicious Palace to invite the Grand Master to the vegetarian tea meeting. The Grand Master walks from the middle of monks towards the left-hand red carpet and turns around to make a bow to monks, then sits on the seat of honor, and the three Grand Khenpos and living Buhhdas are seated in the two rows. At this time, the cook of the Tantra Institute Larang carries a wooden plate in hands, the tea monks of the Medicine Institute and Kalachakra Institute offer tea from the Grand Master to others in turn, and the New Auspicious Larang Palace supplies fried cake, eight-treasure rice and fruits etc. Monks in the whole temple carry tea bowls, chant pre-tea scripture and then drink tea together happily. After drinking tea, the Grand Larang invites everyone to go to Grand Jiwa to have a meal; the three Khenpos and monk officials take out Hadas which are prepared in advance and offer them to the Grand Master for congratulation, and then go to Grand Jiwa to have a meal. Monk meal doesn't mean feast of delicacies from land and sea, but mainly include vegetarian buns such as fried cakes, steamed twisted rolls, sweets, assorter teas mountain, rice and boiled mutton. Boiled mutton is divided according to identity, each common monk can get one piece, while the Grand Master and the Grand Living Buddha can have several pieces.

On the second day of the first month, Grand Jiwa prepares tea and food treatment. The Dharmapala Seance Ceremony is held in the Grand Dharmapala Hall (the Small Golden Tiled Hall) on this day, two Grand Lajis and Dharmapala masters offer "Dianjia" (which is a plate of sweets, food, grape and red dates etc.) and Hadas to the Grand Master when he comes to the Dharmapala Hall, and monks chant *Luosangjiawama Sutra*. After the chanting,

各活佛分列两排就座。这时密宗学院拉让的炊事员手捧木盘，医明和时轮学院的行茶僧从大法台开始依次献茶，拉让吉祥新宫供应油炸果、八宝米饭、果品等。全寺僧人手端茶碗，念诵一段茶前经文，开始用茶，欢聚一堂。茶毕，大拉让请大家到大吉哇赴宴，此时，三大堪布和僧官拿出事先准备好的哈达，依次献给大法台表示祝贺，之后去大吉哇赴宴。所说僧宴，并非是什么丰盛的山珍海味，七碟八碗的宴席，主要是油炸果和花卷等素馍、糖果、茶山、米饭、手抓羊肉。手抓羊肉也按其身份分成份子，普通僧人每人只有一份，大法台和大活佛可分到几份。

大年初二那天，由大吉哇准备茶食宴请。这天在大护法神殿（小金瓦殿）内举行护法神降神仪式，大法台到护法神殿时，两大喇吉、护法神师给大法台献典加（盛一盘糖果、食品、葡萄、红枣等称典加）和哈达，僧众念《罗桑加哇玛经》。诵经完毕，执事僧手执点燃的一撮线香在殿内巡香。两大喇吉给护法神敬献供品，大拉让吉祥新宫给护法神殿献以一套马鞍为主的贺年敬神礼品13种，大吉哇献以一匹缎子为主的礼品11种，六小喇吉献礼各5种，各执事僧官献哈达1条。献礼毕，僧众齐声诵《生死轮回贺涅槃寂静经》及《丹巴玛经》。之后开始降神，护法神师发神占卜新的一年中佛教诸事及其他相关事宜。

初三日为隆波护法殿降神之日，其仪式与大护法殿一样。降神之后，由隆波护法神殿设宴招待参加降神仪式的僧人。

从初三日至初八日之间，由三大学院的六执事僧各茶食宴请僧众。期间僧人用白纸（表示洁白纯净）包上一包砂糖或葡萄干，下垫一张方形红纸（表示喜庆），上盖哈达给自己的上师、老师拜年。老师用奶茶招待，还用红枣、柿饼或梨附原哈

the hierodeacon carries a burning incense stick to cruise incense in the hall. Two grand Lajis sacrifice offerings to Dharmapala, the Grand Larang New Auspicious Palace offers thirteen kinds of presents for New Year and god worshipping, which mainly contains a set of saddle, the Grand Jiwa offers eleven kinds of presents which mainly contains a satin, six small Lajis offer five kinds of presents, and each hierodeacon offers a piece of Hada. After the offering, monks chant *Metempsychosis and Nirvana Sutra* and *Danbama Sutra*. After the starting of seance, the Dharmapala masters tell fortunes of Buddhism and other relevant affairs for the coming year.

The third day is the seance day of the Longbo Dharmapalas Hall, and its ceremony is the same as the Dharmapalas Hall. After the seance, the Longbo Dharmapalas Hall arranges a feast for monks participating in the seance ceremony.

Six hierodeacons coming from the three institutions offer tea and food to entertain monks from the third day to the eighth day. During the period, monks wrap a package of granulated sugar or raisin with a piece of white paper, a piece of square red paper (representing joy) is placed underneath it, and Hadas are placed upon it, which are presents for their masters and teachers. Teachers entertain them with milk tea, and send red dates and dried persimmons or pears with original Hadas to them as presents in return. Tibetans have the convention that presents must be sent to visiting guests for New Year, and they return with presents.

During the festival, monks go out with a package of present (a small package of white sugar, red dates, dried persimmons and raisins) and a piece of Hada, say "Happy New Year" to intimates and exchange presents and Hada with them, and also have the habit of sending presents and treating them. Living Buddhas send presents and pay New Year calls mutually and they believe that courtesy demands reciprocity.

Tibetan New Year activities are completed basically on the eighth day, and preparation works for New Year Grand Prayer Ceremony start.

达回礼。藏族中有给前来拜年送礼的客人必回赐礼品，不让空包回去的习俗。

节日期间，僧人外出怀中揣着一包礼品（如白糖、红枣、柿饼、葡萄干之类的小包）和一条哈达，逢相好者互祝新年好，并交换礼品和哈达，也有相互送礼请客的习惯。活佛之间也相互送礼拜年，礼尚往来十分频繁。

到初八日，藏历新年活动基本结束，开始准备新年祈愿大法会的准备工作。

第三章 藏历年期间的庆祝活动

　　在前面的章节当中，已经介绍了关于藏历年的历史，特别是拉萨人过藏历年的整个过程和习俗。不过，在藏地，过藏历年并不仅仅只是一个家庭的聚会和仪式那么简单，人们还会举行各种各样的活动和仪式来庆祝这个一年当中最隆重的节日。在这个章节当中，将重点介绍藏历年中一些特别有意义的仪式与民间娱乐活动，让读者更加广泛地了解藏历年的习俗。

Chapter Three

Celebrations during Tibetan New Year

The previous chapters have introduced the history of Tibetan New Year, especially the whole process and conventions of Lhasa people's celebration on Tibetan New Year. However, Tibetan New Year celebration isn't as simple as a family union and ceremony, and people hold various kinds of activities and ceremonies to celebrate the grandest festival of a year. This chapter will focus on the introduction of some ceremonies and folk entertainment activities to let readers know about conventions of Tibetan New Year.

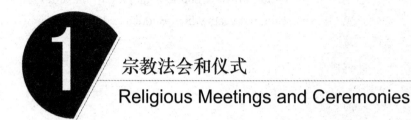

宗教法会和仪式
Religious Meetings and Ceremonies

1. Prayer Ceremony and Ghee Lantern Festival

一、传召法会和酥油灯会

The annual Tibetan New Year Grand Prayer Ceremony is the most important religious festival, and is the extension of a Grand Prayer Ceremony held in Lhasa by Tsongkhapa in 1409, who was the founder of Gelug Sect. The Grand Prayer Ceremony has been held for twenty one days continuously since about the fourth day of the first month. It's said that the Grand Prayer Ceremony came from ancient India, and was the activity to commemorate Sakyamuni who conquered all heresies. It was held for fifteen days originally, and Tsongkhapa added new contents and extended it to twenty-one days. Some Buddhists once believed that the history of Buddha was shortened by five hundred years because Sakyamuni accepted women and inferior people as followers. After Tsongkhapa led Gelug

　　每年藏历年传召大法会是西藏最为重要的宗教节日，由格鲁派的创始人宗喀巴于1409年在拉萨发起的一次祈愿大法会延续而来。传召大法会通常从正月初四左右开始，一直持续二十一天。传说大祈愿法会来源于古印度，当初是为了纪念释迦年尼征服了所有的异端而举行的活动。本来持续十五天，后来宗喀巴附加了新的内涵才延长至二十一天。因为曾有佛教徒相信，由于释迦年尼接受妇女和下等人为信徒，使佛陀的寿命缩短了五百年。宗喀巴带领格鲁派建立三大寺以后，在大昭寺献给释迦牟尼一顶王冠（加顶）作为报答，并延长了大祈愿法会的时间，希望借此补足佛陀损失掉的五百年。

　　传召大法会时，拉萨三大寺僧众聚集到一起诵经祈福。而大法会期间的高潮则是每年正月十五举行的酥油灯会。酥油灯节，又称摆花节、花灯节，藏语是"坚俄曲巴"，非常像汉族正月十五的元宵灯会。有人认为这有可能是宗喀巴受了内地人在正月十五举行元宵灯会的影响。在酥油灯节这一天，白天，人们云集寺院，转经；夜晚，集合于拉萨八廓街，其他市镇的人们则集合于本地的寺前广场，搭起各种花架，有的高达一二十米，层峦叠嶂，上面摆满五彩酥油捏塑的花卉、图案和各种人物、鸟兽，尤以佛、菩萨、供养天女和高僧形象为多；还有一些是成屏连片的，讲述了佛传

Sect to set up the three temples, he offered a crown to Sakyamuni to repay him and extended the time of the Grand Prayer Ceremony, hoping to make up for five hundred years which Buddha had lost.

Monks of the three temples of Lhasa get together, chant and pray during the Grand Prayer Ceremony. During the climax of the Grand Ceremony, Ghee Lantern Festival is held on the fifteenth day of the first month every year. Ghee Lantern Festival is also called Festival of Flowers or Lantern Festival, and its Tibetan is "Jian'e Quba", which is similar to Lantern Festival of Han people held on the fifteenth day of the first month. Some people thought that the reason may be that Tsongkhapa was influenced by Lantern Festival held by inner land people on the fifteenth day of the first month. On the Ghee Lantern Festival, people get together in the temples to pray in the daytime; they assemble in Eight Barkhor Street of Lhasa at night, and people in other cities and towns gather on the local squares to set up various kinds of flower stands. Some of the stands are as high as ten or twenty meters, and images of flowers, patterns, figures, birds, beasts, and especially Buddhas, Bodhisattvas, goddesses, great monks made of colorful ghee are placed on the stands layer upon layer; and some of the stands tell about Buddhist stories, myths and legends cohesively. After flower lanterns are lighted, they are so splendid that they look like bright stars. People hold a carnival with the flower lanterns all night.

There are many different legends about ghee flowers and Ghee Lantern festival which are circulated in Tibetan areas. One version was that Princess Wencheng brought a Sakyamuni statue when she went to Tibet, and scarified it to a temple after she arrived in Tibet. Tibetans wanted to offer a bunch of flowers to express their gratitude to the princess and their respect to Buddha, but there were no flowers in the winter, they had to make flowers with edible ghee, so ghee flowers were made afterwards.

Another version was that the great master Tsongkhapa held the Grand Prayer Ceremony of ten thousand monks in Lhasa in the first month of 1409. He dreamed that weeds and dead woods became flowers, thorns turned into bright lights, and thousands of treasures glowed among bright lights and flowers, which were so beautiful and magnificent. When he woke up, he organized monks to carve images and offered them to Buddhas in order to represent his dream. Therefore, Ghee Lantern Festival is held on the night of the fifteenth day of the first month every year, and it is the important content of the Grand Ceremony in the first month.

故事和神话传说。花灯点燃后，犹如群星闪烁，一片辉煌。人们在花灯下彻夜狂欢。

关于酥油花和酥油灯会还有好多不同的传说流传在藏区。一种是说相传当年文成公主进藏时携带了一尊释迦牟尼佛像，到西藏后供奉在寺院当中，藏人为了表达对公主的感谢和对佛的崇敬，想献上一束鲜花，可是当时正值寒冷冬季，无花可摘，便只好用食用的酥油塑成鲜花献在佛前，从此便有了酥油花。

另一种是说1409年的正月，宗喀巴大师在拉萨举办万名僧侣参加的盛大祈愿法会。有天晚上，大师梦见满地杂草枯木变成了鲜花，荆棘变成了明灯，在明灯鲜花之间千千万万颗珍宝在闪烁，极其美丽壮观。大师醒来以后为了再现梦境，便组织僧众用酥油雕塑，塑成后供在佛前。所以每年正月十五日夜要举行酥油花灯会，是正月大法会的重要内容。

在整个藏区内，最好的酥油花雕塑艺术展是在宗喀巴的出生地——青海的塔尔寺。当地人对这天极为重视，为了那一个晚上的奢华陈列，常常要耗费塔尔寺僧众和众多艺术家几个月的心血。塔尔寺的宗教艺术品以堆绣、壁画和酥油花最有代表性，称为"艺术三绝"，而酥油花又居三绝之首。

酥油花从西藏传入塔尔寺，僧人们为了更好地再现宗喀巴大师的梦境，专门设立了上下花院，有专职的工艺僧人研究制作，相互竞赛。每年的农历十月开始，两院艺人便开始精心制作，从设计图案到调和酥油，扎绑框架，调色捏塑，描金绘饰，都十分讲究。平常两院互相保密，连僧人也很少往来。直到正月十五夜，两院才一齐拿出他们的作品，让僧俗群众评论优劣。这种竞争使僧人们竭尽心智创新，并借鉴其他民族和民间的雕塑艺术手法，与佛教艺术巧妙地融合在一起，因而创作技

In the entire Tibetan areas, the best Ghee Flower Sculpture Exhibition is held in Ta'er Temple in Qinghai, the birthplace of Tsongkhap. Local people attach great importance to this day, and it often takes several months for monks of Ta'er Temple and many artists to prepare for luxurious exhibition of that night. Religious artworks are represented by barbola, mural and ghee flower, which are called "three perfect artworks", and ghee flower ranks No. 1 among these three artworks.

Ghee flowers are passed from Tibet to Ta'er Temple, monks set up upper and lower flower houses especially, and professional artistic monks do research and make them and compete with one another. Since the tenth month in each lunar calendar year, artists in the two houses begin to make ghee flowers delicately, and particular attentions are paid to designing patters, mixing ghee, binding frameworks, toning, moulding, gilding and painting. The two houses often keep secrets from each other, and monks have little contact with the other. The two houses don't present their works till the night on the fifteenth day of the first month, and ask monks and common people to comment on inferiority and superiority. This kind of competition drives monks to make efforts to innovate, borrow other national and folk sculpture methods, integrate with Buddhist arts delicately, so their creation skills become more refined and unique world-famous sculpture arts are formed finally. In early 1991, ghee flowers of Ta'er Temple were exhibited in Beijing and won great acclaim. Therefore, annual Ta'er Temple Ghee Lantern Festival attracts tens of thousands of pilgrims and tourists, and some of them come to worship Buddha and go sightseeing from Tibet, Sichuan, Gansu and Inner Mongolia. There is a famous poem which describes ghee lanterns specially:

"The moon is in the sky, and tinkles of *xiao* and drums are heard. Light stands are arranged in decorated tends, and flowers are different every year. Lanterns glow solemnly and magnificently, figures are so vivid, and buildings are exquisite. Strange and vivid forms show wonderful workmanship of monks."

However, the entire activity in Lhasa or Ta'er Temple was like a dream and must end before daybreak in the past. When the first sunbeam shone the land, such delicate and fine artworks must be destroyed without a trace, which aimed at letting people understand the theme of Buddhism and know that life was ephemeral and dream-like emptiness had no sense. At present, ghee lanterns of Ta'er Temple will be stored and displayed after the exhibition of that night of the fifteenth day of the first month, so that tourists can appreciate them on ordinary occasions.

艺越来越精湛，终于形成了独树一帜、驰名中外的雕塑艺术。1991年初，塔尔寺的酥油花进京展出，赢得了好评。所以塔尔寺的酥油花灯节每年吸引香客游人数以万计，其中有不少是从西藏、四川、甘肃、内蒙古专程赶过去拜佛观光的。有一首很有名的诗是专门描绘酥油花灯的：

"月当空，耳边箫鼓叮咚。彩棚间安排灯架，年年花样不同。放光明，庄严灿烂，肖人物，楼阁玲珑。怪怪奇奇，形形色色，番僧巧夺天工。"

不过，在过去，不管是在拉萨还是塔尔寺，整个活动就像一场梦，必须在黎明前结束。当第一束阳光照耀大地的时候，如此多精美绝伦的艺术品都必须销毁，不留一点痕迹。这为的是让大家深刻领会佛教的宗旨，人生不过是昙花一现，空幻如梦没有更多的意义。如今，塔尔寺的酥油花在元宵夜展出过后会保存陈列，平常可以供游人欣赏。

2. Festival of Dance to Gods

Ghost Driving Ceremony is hold all over Lhasa from the temples to houses of common people on the twenty-ninth day of the twelfth month. As for the temples in Lhasa, Ghost Driving Ceremony is also a very important memorial ceremony on this day. The temples in Lhasa usually hold the grand ceremony of dance to gods to pray peace in the coming year on this day, so they usually call it Festival of Dance to Gods. Dance to gods is called "Qiangmu" in Tibetan, and is a kind of religious ceremonial dance performed by Lamas and monks when ceremonies and celebrations are held in the temples in the Tibetan areas. It's said that this kind of religious dance aiming at "driving ghosts and dispelling evils" was introduced from India and Nepal to Tibet in the Tang Dynasty, i.e. the seventh century, and Tibetan monks integrated Tibetan wind dance, witch dance of Bonism and mask god dance of Indian Yogacara. It was performed successfully at the cornerstone ceremony of Samye Temple, and became the embryonic form of the primitive "Qiangmu". Another saying was that it was created by the master of Tantrism Padma Sambhava, and the main content was to vanquish demons and monsters and promote Dharma.

二、跳神节

在拉萨，腊月二十九这天从上到下，从寺院到寻常百姓家里通常都要进行驱鬼仪式。而对拉萨的各大寺院来说，这一天的驱鬼仪式也是一个重要的宗教祭奠仪式。在这一天，拉萨各大寺院通常会进行隆重的跳神仪式来驱鬼，以祈求来年平安，所以他们通常又把这一天称为跳神节。跳神，藏语称为"羌姆"，是藏区各寺庙举行法会庆典时通常都会进行的一种由喇嘛僧侣表演的宗教仪式舞蹈。这种舞蹈，据说是唐朝，即公元七世纪，佛教从印度、尼泊尔传入西藏的过程当中，藏族僧侣将西藏的上风舞、苯教的巫舞与印度瑜伽派的面具神舞相结合，创造的一种以"驱鬼镇邪"为主旨的宗教舞蹈，并在桑耶寺的奠基仪式上表演获得成功，成为原始"羌姆"的雏形。还有一种说法是八世纪的时候由佛教密宗大师莲花生首创，内容主要是表现降魔伐妖，弘扬佛法。

"羌姆"有单人舞、双人舞和集体舞三种形式。跳舞时戴假面具，穿长袍，配彩带和刀盾。伴奏的乐器有舞钹、牛角号、唢呐等。面具是最有特色的，多为立体雕刻面具，也有少量的平面布面具，通常除了佛像、菩萨像、历代高僧圣人像之外，更多的是表现"益西巴"和"吉德巴"两大类邪法中的各类神仙鬼怪，即护法神灵，这些护法神灵的职责是护卫佛法和修行佛法的人。护法神繁多，神祇多为佛或者菩萨的化身，在造型上多为身着骷髅花蔓或缠绕毒蛇，常以人头骨、心脏、鲜血为装饰，被称为"本尊护法神"。还有一些护法神的面相狰狞，或血口大开，或怒目圆睁，或龇牙，或卷舌。但跳神面具无论是善相还是恶相都是宗教内容的反映，所以如果脱离寺院和宗教祭奠将无从理解它的内涵和意义。

当跳神开始的时候，首先举行献祭仪式，场上

"Qiangmu" has three forms, single-person dance, double-person dance and collective dance. When dancing, people wear masks and gowns with colorful stripes, and hold knives and shields. The musical accompaniments include dance cymbals, bullhorns and *suona* etc. Masks have the most distinctive characteristic, most of which are three-dimensional carved masks, and a few of which are two-dimensional cloth masks. They represent images of Buddhas, Bodhisattvas, great monks and sages of past dynasties, as well as various kinds of fairies and demons, who are Dharmapalas and are responsible for guarding Dharma and people practicing Dharma. There are a large variety of Dharmapalas, which are embodiments of Buddhas or Bodhisattvas, and are often called "Yidam Dharmapalas" decorated by human skulls, hearts and blood and accompanied by sheleton flower vines or poisonous snakes. Some Dharmapalas have ugly faces, or bloody mouths, or big staring eyes, or long teeth, or rolling tongues. However, dancing masks reflect religious contents regardless of whether they are good or evil, so its connotations and meaning cannot be understood without temples and religious foundations.

When the dance to gods starts, the sacrifice ceremony is held at first, drums and cymbals are beating together on the stage, iron-rod Lamas leading the honor guard appear on the stage, then guardian warriors with black hats, Dharmapalas, monsters, human skeletons walk one after another, "gods and monsters" get together, dance and march around the stage, and then dance episodes are performed consecutively. "Qiangmu" has many independent dance episodes, such as demon dance, skeleton dance, Bull God dance, guardian warrior dance, Dharmapala dance and so on. These dances are often accompanied with instrumental rhythms slowly. At last, demons and monsters kneel on the ground together, which symbolizes that they are vanquished and are converted to Buddhists. It's thought that "Qiangmu" reflects the struggle process of Buddhism and Bonism, and praises success of Buddhism respectfully. Besides struggles between Buddhism and evils, some Buddhist stories are also performed, such as "Prince Shaduona who fed a tiger with his body" and "feeding eagles with flesh" etc. On the twenty-ninth day of the twelfth month, the temples of Lamaism of Tibetan GeLug Sect such as the Jokhang Temple, Mulu Temple and the Potala Palace etc. hold the grand ceremony of dance to gods in Lhasa, all the highest deacons, living Buddhas and Khenpos of the temples of Lamaism of Tibetan Gelug Sect participate in it, and countless common people and followers are attracted to watch it, and it becomes a watching focus to attract Chinese and foreign tourists to Tibet, and there is a sea of people on the scene. Therefore, many secular contents are added into dance to gods in the later

鼓号、铙钹齐鸣，先由铁棒喇嘛带领仪仗队出场，然后黑帽金刚、各护法神、鬼怪、骷髅依次鱼贯而行，众"神怪"聚集，缓缓起舞，绕场一周，然后相继演出舞蹈片段。"羌姆"有很多独立的舞蹈片段，诸如凶神舞、骷髅舞、牛神舞、金刚力士舞、护法神舞，等等。跳这些舞的时候跟着乐器的节奏跳动，通常都比较缓慢。到最后，恶魔精怪一齐跪在地上，表示均被降伏而皈依佛法。有人认为"羌姆"是反映了佛教与苯教的斗争过程，是对佛教胜利的礼赞。除了表现佛教与邪恶的斗争，通常还会演出一些佛教故事，譬如有"萨哆那太子舍身伺虎"、"割肉喂鹰"等故事。在拉萨，腊月二十九那天，大昭寺、木鹿寺、布达拉宫等黄教寺院都要举行跳神仪式，场面非常隆重，不仅黄教各大寺院的最高执事、活佛、堪布等都要参加，还会吸引无数老百姓、信徒前来观看，如今更成为吸引到藏区旅游的中外游客的一大看点，场面常常是人山人海。所以，到后期跳神内容也加入很多世俗的内容，如寿星舞，还穿插摔跤、角斗等嬉戏场面，以娱乐大众。

　　"跳神"随着藏传佛教在整个藏区的传播，也从拉萨传到藏区的其他地方。但是各地各派因其信奉的本尊和护法神有所不同，因而举行跳神的日期、程序、舞蹈、服饰也有所不同，譬如日喀则地区的跳神节大概就在每年的藏历八月。而且不同地方对"跳神"的称呼也不太一样，譬如在北京雍和宫的跳神叫做"跳布扎"；云南、四川藏区叫"麻羌"；青海叫"跳钎"；内蒙古则叫"查玛"。虽然叫法不一样，但是都含有驱鬼迎祥之意，实际上都是西藏"羌姆"的传承、演变和发展。

period such as birthday star dance, wrestling and fighting etc. in order to entertain the masses.

"Dance to gods" are spread from Lhasa to other areas with the spreading of Tibetan Buddhism in the entire Tibetan areas. However, different Yidams and Dharmapalas are followed by different schools in different areas, so dates, procedures, dances, clothes for dance to gods are also different. For example, in Shigatse, dance to gods is held in every August of Tibetan calendar. Besides dates, names are also varied. Dance to gods is called "dancing Buzha" in Yonghe Palace, "Maqiang" in the Tibetan areas in Yunnan and Sichuan, "Tiaoqian" in Qinghai, and "Chama" in Inner Mongolia. Although the names are different, they have the meaning of driving ghosts and welcoming luck, and are the inheritance, evolution and development of Tibetan "Qiangmu".

2 民间娱乐活动
Folk Entertainment Activities

一、节日贺词和民歌

藏历年贺词

节日期间的藏人总是特别热情、快乐和亢奋。在藏历年期间，人们见面不管藏族还是汉族，中国人还是外国人，认识的还是不认识的人都要互道吉祥如意的节日贺词，他们常用的新年贺词有：

"扎西德勒"——吉祥如意！

"洛萨尔桑"——新年好！

"扎西德勒彭松措"——晚辈祝福老人：

1. Festival Congratulations and Folk Songs

Congratulations on Tibetan New Year

Tibetans are especially enthusiastic, happy and excited during festivals. In the period of Tibetan New Year, people will say happy and lucky festival congratulations one another no matter they are Tibetans or Han people, Chinese or foreigners, and no matter whether they know each other or not, and there are their common New Year congratulations:

"Tashi Delek"——Good luck and fortune!

"Luosa Ersang"——Happy New Year!

"Tashi Delek Pengsongcuo"—— The junior blesses the senior: Good luck, happiness and boundless beneficence!

"Ama Bazhu Gongkangsang"—— Wish the hostess health and longevity!

"Dingduo Dewa Tubaxiu"—— Wish you peace and luck every year!

"Nanyang Zongju Yuebaxiu"—— May we can get together like this every year!

"Jiji! Suosuo! Lajiluo!"—— May god endow happiness and peace!

"Xiapuda"—— Cheers!

Toast Songs

Besides mutual congratulations, people throw barley, express good wishes, drink wine, sing songs and dance one another. On the second day of the first month, enthusiasm and happiness of Tibetans can be felt when they pay New Year calls. They like paying New Year calls collectively, and enjoy bustle and excitement, wine and songs. The whole family or household or company or industry pays New Year visits, sometimes children pay New Year visits together, sometimes young people pay New Year visits together, and sometimes old men or old women pay New Year visits together. Toasts shall be proposed when people pay New Year calls, and they shall sing toast songs and play Tibetan operas

吉祥如意，功德无量！

"阿妈巴珠工康桑"——愿女主人健康长寿！

"顶多德瓦土巴秀"——愿岁岁平安吉利！

"南央宗聚悦巴秀"——愿年年这样欢聚！

"吉吉！索索！拉结罗！"——祈求神灵赐予幸福和平安！

"下普达"——干杯！

祝酒歌

除了相互恭贺，还要互相扬撒青稞祝福，相互喝酒、唱歌甚至踏歌起舞。特别在正月初二拜年的时候，尤其能感觉到藏族人的热情和快乐。他们拜年喜欢集体行动，喜欢热热闹闹，喜欢有酒有歌。或者全家出动，或者整个院落出动，整个单位出动，或者整个行业出动，有时小孩结伴拜年，有时是年轻人结伴拜年，有时是老阿爸或者是老阿妈结伴拜年。拜年的时候必会敬酒，敬酒的时候必会唱酒歌、唱藏戏。这时就算平常走路东倒西歪的老人，在这种场合之下，每每唱歌起舞，饮酒干杯，也顿时会精神焕发，满面红光，周身洋溢青春的活力。如若你身在他们中间，一定会为他们的热情、快乐、幸福所打动，跟着他们踏歌起舞。

歌、舞、酒对藏人来说已经不仅仅是他们的娱乐方式，而已成为他们日常生活的有机组成部分。不管是否在节日，随时随地，只要他们感到快乐，就会随之唱歌和舞蹈，以此来表达他们心中热烈的情感。节日期间更是如此，在任何场景下面，拜年的时候，劝酒的时候，游戏的时候，甚至干活的时候，他们都能够随口以歌踏舞来相互交流，相互传达情感。他们的歌谣真诚朴实，而又热情奔放。譬如，在乡下，小孩子们成群结队地跑到人家家里面去拜年，就要唱祝福歌：

祝主人的庄稼今年大丰收，

when toasts are proposed. On this occasion, even old staggering men are full of energy and youthful vitality and look refreshed. If you stay among them, you will be touched by their enthusiasm and happiness, sing songs and dance with them.

As for Tibetans, songs, dance and wine are their entertainment methods as well as organic components in their daily life. Whether there is a festival or not, they will sing songs and dance to express their strong feelings if they feel happy at any time and in any place. They sing songs and dance casually to communicate with one another and convey their emotions during festivals or on any occasions, such as when they pay New Year calls, when they propose toasts, when they play games, or even when they work. Their songs are sincere, simple and enthusiastic. For example, children run to others' houses to pay New Year calls in groups and sing a benediction song:

I hope that the master has a good harvest,

The barley will be as big as a pigeon,

The pea pod will be as long as an arm,

The rape will be as high as a bamboo,

One-year grains cannot be eaten up in ten years.

When people meet, they propose toasts mutually, and sing toast songs when proposing toasts. If you don't drink three cups consecutively, they will not let you go; if you refuse to drink, they will sing enthusiastic toast or persuasion songs till you drink.

I propose a toast to you,
A cup of wine is made from fine barley,
I hope that you can drink it up,
Please don't reject it.

Don't drink wine so fast,

Drinking wine differs from drinking water,

Don't sing a song so fast,

Singing songs differs from quarreling;

Don't dance so fast,

Dancing differs from making iron.

种出的青稞有鸽子那么大，

种出的豆荚有手臂那么长，

种出的油菜有竹子那么高，

一年的粮食十年也吃不完。

和别人见面的时候，相互敬酒，边敬酒还要边唱祝酒歌，通常如果你不连喝三杯是不会放你走的，如果你一再推辞，他们就会唱热情洋溢的敬酒歌或者劝酒歌，直到你把酒喝下去为止。

敬上一杯青稞酒，
上等青稞把它酿，
我只愿你畅饮尽，
千万千万别推让。
酒，不要催快喝快喝，

喝酒跟饮驴不一样；
歌，不要催快唱快唱，

唱歌跟吵架不一样；
舞，不要催快跳快跳，

跳舞跟打铁不一样。

喝酒不唱歌，
跟毛驴饮水差不多。

　　如果是家庭朋友聚会的酒宴，在酒宴席上的讲究就更多了。以前人的长幼尊卑区分得非常严格，现在没有那么严格的讲究，但是一般酒宴上，座次也有一些规矩。酒宴一般分为首席、次席、末席三个档次。坐在首席的人，大都是年高的长者或者尊贵的客人，陪坐末席的，往往是年纪最小、辈分最低的人。所有的人坐定后，酒女们便会开始唱：

四柱八梁的房子，
汇聚着亲密的朋友；
喝着甜香的美酒，
唱起动人的酒歌。

高山纯净的雪水，
家乡白色的青稞；
酿出醇香的好酒，
胜过神仙的甘露。

香甜的美酒酿好了，
亲密的人儿汇齐了；

Drinking wine without singing,
Is the same as a donkey which drinks water.

Particular attentions shall be paid to banquets for parties of family members and friends. There were sharp distinctions among the senior, the junior, the superior and the inferior in the past, while the rules aren't as strict as the previous ones, while there are some rules for seats. Banquet often has three classes, the seats of honor, the inferior seats and the least prominent seats. The seats of honor are for the senior or honored guests, and the least prominent seats are for the junior and the inferior. After all the people are seated, the wine maids begin to sing:

Close friends get together,
In the house with four columns and eight beams;
They are drinking sweet, fragrant and fine wine,
And singing pleasant toast songs.

Pure snow water from mountains,
White hometown barley,
Are the materials of fragrant and fine wine,
Which is better than the sweet dew of immortals.

Sweet and fine wine has been made,
Close friends get together,

People are so happy and wine is so sweet,

It's a pleasant time to drink.

When toasts are proposed to the senior and the honored guest, the corresponding toast songs shall be sang. For example:

Cups of fine barley wine,

Are offered to the seated senior.

They become drunk slightly,

The whole house becomes brilliant.

The gold gourds are filled with fine wine,

They are offered to the honored guests;

The gold gourds are so splendid,

The guests are so healthy.

Please drink wine comfortably,

Please sing songs happily;

Comfortable and happy time,

Is better than a hundred ounces of gold.

After toasts are proposed to the senior and honored guests, and many toast songs are sung, the banquet environment becomes strong and vivid gradually, and people begin to propose toasts and sing toast songs one another, who are in the similar ages and positions in the family hierarchy, and pay no particular attention to etiquette. Toasts are divided into "Jueqiang", "Guoqiang", "Tiqiang" and "Xiuqiang". The best performance is that singing and drinking are synchronously, that is when wine is drunk up, the song is over. "Jueqiang" means

人欢聚，酒甜香，

是开怀畅饮的时光。

给长者、贵宾敬酒时，要唱相应的酒歌。譬如：

斟满青稞美酒，

献给上座的长辈。

长辈喝得微微醉，

四座充盈了光辉。

金瓢盛满了好酒，

敬献尊贵的客人；

金瓢多么辉煌，

客人多么健康。

请舒舒服服喝酒，

请快快乐乐歌唱；

舒服快乐时光，

胜过黄金百两。

随着酒宴的进行，敬过了长者，敬过了嘉宾，敬过客人，唱了很多祝酒歌后，酒宴的氛围越渐浓厚和活跃，便开始到了互相敬酒、互唱酒歌的时候。大都是年龄相近、辈分相同，互相没有那么多礼节的人们。这时的敬酒分为"觉羌""果羌""梯羌""休羌"多

种。最佳表现是酒歌与喝
酒同步，歌唱完，酒饮
干。"觉羌"意思是快
酒，酒歌还没有唱完，酒
已经喝完了，这样要罚
酒；"果羌"意为慢酒，
酒歌唱完了，还在磨磨蹭
蹭，不肯痛痛快快地喝，
也要挨罚；"梯羌"意为
剩酒，把酒虽喝完，酒盅
里还有剩余的酒滴，这样
的人更要挨罚，重新再喝
一盅。这时相互之间唱的
酒歌曲调更加丰富,歌词更
俏皮、活泼、有趣：

少男少女聚一堂，
饮酒欢歌喜洋洋；
不识时务的死神呵，
赶快滚到一旁！.

要么我来敬你酒，
我唱一首酒歌；
要么你来敬我酒，
你唱一首酒歌。

好酒你来喝，
酒歌我来唱；
酒和酒歌，
没有消停的时光。
很想唱一支酒歌，
可惜嗓子嘶哑；
嗓子嘶哑不要紧，

fast drinking, a person drinks up wine before a song is over, he or she will be penalized another cup of wine; "Guoqiang" means a person refuses to drink joyfully when a song is over, he or she will be penalized; "Tiqiang" means surplus drinking, a person drinks up wine, but there is surplus drops in the cup, he or she will be penalized to drink another cup. By this time, tunes of toast songs become richer, and words become smarter, more vivid and interesting:

Young people get together,
They drink wine and sing songs happily;
Death, you lack proper understanding,
Get out of here quickly!

I propose a toast to you,
I sing a toast song;
Or you propose a toast to me,
You sing a toast song.

You drink fine wine,
I sing a toast song,
With wine and songs,
We have a non-stop revelry.
I really want to sing a toast song,
But I have a coarse throat;
It doesn't matter to sing coarsely,

It's more pleasant to sing a coarse song.

Drink a cup of fine wine,
Enjoy yourself with it;
Please don't pour delicious wine,
It's such a pity to pour it.

During festivals, people like participating in various kinds of wine parties for revelry, which often last a long time; if people get together in the morning, they leave in the evening; if they get together in the afternoon, they leave at midnight, and sometimes they hold a wine party all night till dawn. Tibetans leave an impression that they like joining rather than being apart, they like cooperation rather than solitude, they like liveliness rather than coldness. Therefore, they are reluctant to leave, embrace cheek to cheek, even cry when parties finish. By this time, they will drink farewell wine, which was called "Xiuqiang" in old times, sing farewell songs, praise good wine parties, and hope that there are more happy reunions in future.

Days in the last year were comfortable,
Days in this year are comfortable too,
I wish days in the next year,
Will be luckier and happier.
Lhasa, Lhasa is comfortable,
Lalu, Lalu is comfortable,

唱支哑歌更动人。

喝上好酒一杯,
肚里添个宝贝;
请别把酒泼洒了,
泼洒宝贝多可惜。

在节日期间人们都喜欢参加各种酒会,聚在一起狂欢,酒会时间总是拖得很长,上午聚会,傍晚才散;下午聚会,深夜才结束,有些甚至通宵达旦。藏人给人的印象是喜聚不喜散,喜欢合群不喜欢孤独,喜欢热闹不喜欢冷清。所以,每当聚会要结束的时候,他们总是显得依依不舍,还要互相拥抱、贴脸,甚至流泪。这时候,他们往往还要喝告别酒,旧时"休羌",还要唱告别歌,赞美当天的酒宴好,祝愿今后有更多的欢聚时光。

去年的日子舒服,
今年的日子也舒服,
但愿明年这个时候,
日子更加吉祥幸福。
拉萨拉萨舒服,
拉鲁拉鲁舒服,

拉萨和拉鲁中间，
龙王潭园林更舒服。
今天的聚会这样欢喜，

为什么还要分离？
今夜的星星如此灿烂，

为什么还要消散？
我们在这里欢聚，
但愿长聚不散；
长聚不散的人们
永无病痛和灾难！

情歌

节日期间通常也是藏族青年男女们在一起聚会玩耍的大好机会。特别是他们常常在新年期间结伴到山地林间玩耍，这时候他们通常要唱一些相互表达爱慕之情的歌谣，藏族有不少恋歌流传很广，歌词常常朴实而深情，这里可以举一首比较有名的恋歌：

女："嗟，我的爱人！设尔为树，植于软土，侬将溪叶，共彼霜露。"

男："云向前行，快

Compared with Lhasa and Lalu,
Dragon King Pool Garden is more comfortable.
The party is so happy today,

Why shall we leave?
The stars are so bright in the sky tonight,

Why shall they disappear?
We get together here,
And wish we will not separate;
People living together;
Will not have diseases, pains and disasters forever!

Love Songs

During festivals, Tibetan young people often grasp the good chance to get together and play. When they go to forests to play, they sing some love songs to express their love each other usually. Many Tibetan love songs have spread far and abroad, and the words are often simple and touching, and I take a very famous love song as example here:

Woman: "Oh, my lover! I regard you as a tree planted in soft soil, you will be a leaf, I will bear frost and dew with you."

Man: "The cloud moves forward, even the fast

horse cannot catch it! We are falling in love, our parents cannot separate us."

Woman: "My heart is like milk without dust; I store it in the jade cup for my beloved."

Man: "I look at those luxurious houses in front of me, not to live in. I stride with my chin up, just like a rooster."

Women: "I want to climb the steep mountains, trek across the deep valleys, and ford the violent storm and torrents with you."

Man: "You wear plain simple dresses, but you are as pretty as a fairy in my eyes. You stand beside a tree, but you are on intimate terms with me."

Woman: "The howling of the dogs can stop pedestrians; the rumor of others cannot prevent me from loving you."

Man: "The mountain is so high, there is a way to climb it; the fountain source keeps primal chaos, so does our pure love."

Woman: "My parents stop me, my relatives insult me, they want me to break with you, but I will not do it. If the hunting dog catches the deer, how can it escape?"

2. "Guoxie" and "Guozhuang"

Besides songs, there are dances. In the Tibetan areas, you can see men and women, the old and the young dancing hand in hand everywhere during festivals, and dances are needed for New

马莫能及也；尔我相爱，父母不能折也。"

女："我心如乳，不染纤尘；贮以玉杯，奉我良人。"

男："幢幢华屋，容我驻足，我如雄鸡，昂冠驰人。"

女："危峰绝谷，与尔跋之。激瀑洪流，与尔涉之。"

男："尔衣荆布，美如宝珍，尔虽木立，能系我心。"

女："有犬狂吠，可阻行人；旁人窃议，无妨尔我之爱情。"

男："高山仰止，有径赴之；源泉混混，进无已时；尔我赴爱，乃亦如之。"

女："父母阻我，亲戚辱我，欲我绝汝，我决不可。猎犬获鹿，其何能脱。"

二、"果谐"与"锅庄"

除了歌，当然少不了舞。在藏族地区，每逢节假日，不论你走到哪里，都可以看见男女老少，拉起手，翩翩起舞，过年时分自然更需要舞蹈来助兴。在牧区，经常举行有趣的篝火晚会，人们通宵达旦唱歌跳舞。在城镇，天气一暖和，人们便阖家外出，在林卡里边喝青稞酒，边跳起民间舞蹈，从早到晚，兴尽而归。

在藏区，最为人所熟知的舞蹈就是"果谐"与"锅庄"，这是流行在所有藏族地区的一种圆圈舞。一般地说，在雅鲁藏布江流域的广大农区，把这种圆圈舞叫"果谐"；在昌都地区及四川、云南等藏区，则称其为"锅庄"。一般分为用于大型宗教祭祀的大"锅庄"，传统节日上一般就是中"锅庄"，亲朋聚会就是小"锅庄"。这种圆圈舞并没有太多形式上和内容上的限制，都是兴之所至，随时随地便可翩翩起舞，最是自由豪放。跳的同时还常常配有歌唱，唱法有长有促，有急有缓，有扬有抑；舞法则举手投足，或进或退，或就地踏歌，或旋转回翔，或匜突

Year entertainment naturally. Interesting bonfire parties are often held in pastoral areas, and people sing songs and dance all night. When it is warm, all family members go out from towns, they drink barley wine in forests and play fork dances from dawn to night and go home happily.

In the Tibetan areas, the well-known dances are "Guoxie" and "Guozhuang", which are a kind of circle dance all over the Tibetan areas. Generally speaking, this kind of circle dance is called "Guoxie" in massive rural area of the Yarlung Zangbo River Valley; and it is called "Guozhuang" in the Tibetan areas such as Qamdo Prefecture, Sichuan, Yunnan and so on. Usually, it can be divided into large "Guozhuang" for large-scale religious sacrifice, medium "Guozhuang" for traditional festivals and small "Guozhuang" for get-together of relatives and friends. This kind of circle dance doesn't have limitations on formalities or contents, which are driven by mood, so people can dance at any time in any place, and they are free and bold. Dance is accompanied by a song, which is long or short, fast or slow, rising or falling; dance changes with rhythms, people move forward or backward, or mark time, or rotate and circle around, or run suddenly. Usually, men and women make a circle hand in hand, one person takes the lead, then men and women ask and answer, and sing in antiphonal style repetitively without accompaniment of musical instruments. The whole dance is divided into two parts from slow tempo to fast tempo, the basic actions include "striding with a swing", "stepping stance and tossing", "striding and squatting" and so on, arms change gestures mainly in the ways of lifting, swinging and shaking, the formation changes in a clockwise direction, the circle is large sometimes and is small sometimes, and turns into the pattern of "dragon wags its tail".

"Guoxie" and "Guozhuang" in the Tibetan areas have their own characteristics, in which "Guozhuang" in Qamdo is the most wonderful and famous. During festival celebrations, men and women get together on squares or in yards, sing and dance in a circle from right to left. Men wear fat and big cuffless trousers, which are like strong hairy legs of eagle, and women take off right sleeve and wrap it around the back, and look graceful and free. Men and women stand on each side, form a circle hand in hand, and some people sing a song and the others join in the chorus. Men often take the lead in singing in unison, and their sound is loud and clear and has strong penetrating power. The dance leader and the composer walk around the circle in the way of "swinging hands and making fluttery steps". When the song lyrics come to an end, the crowd cry together the sound of "ya", and then suddenly the dancers cast out their arms to the sides rapidly, twist at the waist, make

奔肆。一般男女各排半圆拉手成圈，有一人领头，分男女一问一答，反复对唱，无乐器伴奏。整个舞蹈由先慢后快的两段舞组成，基本动作有"悠颤跨腿"、"趋步辗转"、"跨腿踏步蹲"等，手臂以撩、甩、晃为主变换舞姿，队形按顺时针行进，圆圈有大有小，偶尔变换"龙摆尾"图案。

藏族地区的"果谐"与"锅庄"各有特色。其中，昌都的"锅庄"最为精彩有名。每逢节日庆典之际，广场上、庭院里，男女相聚，围成圆圈，自右而左，边歌边舞。男性穿着肥大筒裤，有如雄鹰粗壮的毛腿，女子脱开右臂袍袖披于身后，飘逸洒脱。男女各站一边，拉手成圈，分班唱和，通常由男性带头启唱，歌声嘹亮、穿透力强，舞群和着歌曲作"甩手颤踏步"沿圈走动，当唱词告一段落后，众人一齐"呀"的一声呼叫，顿时加快速度，撒开双臂侧身拧腰大搓步跳起，挥舞双袖载歌载舞，奔跑跳跃变化动作，尤以男性动作幅度较大，伸展双臂有如雄鹰盘旋奋飞。女性动作幅度较小，点步转圈有如凤凰摇翅飞舞、健美、明快而活泼。舞圈中央通常置青稞酒、哈达，舞毕由长者或组织者敬献美酒、哈达。"果谐"、"锅庄"之所以在藏区受到广泛的欢迎和喜爱，就是因为男女老少皆可随意参加，不受时间、地点、人数的限制，形式也相当奔放、自由、活泼，能够充分将藏人的热情、奔放、快乐的情怀淋漓尽致地表现出来。如今只要在节日庆典到藏区旅行的人都会被热情的藏人邀请加入他们的"果谐"和"锅庄"舞蹈，即使不会舞蹈的人也会被他们那热烈的氛围感染而跟着他们一起踏歌起舞。

large stumbling steps, and leap. They wave sleeves, singing and dancing, running and leaping as they make different movements. Men's movements are featured by large movement range: both arms stretch out widely, like eagles' circling and soaring. Women's movements are characterized by smaller movement range: they make small steps as they turn in circles, like a phoenix, wings trembling in flight. The dance reveals strong and handsome, lively and spirited features. Generally, barley wine and Hada, a ceremonial scarf, are placed in the center of dance circle. At the end of the performance, the elder or organizers will respectfully present the wine and Hada. The reason why "Guoxie" and "Guozhuang" are widely popular among people in the Tibetan areas is that men and women, the young and old can participate in them, aren't limited by time, place and number, forms are rather bold, free and lively, and can fully represent enthusiasm, boldness and happiness of Tibetans. At present, people who travel in the Tibetan areas during festival celebrations will be invited by enthusiastic Tibetans to join in their "Guoxie" and "Guozhuang" dances, even people who aren't good at dancing will be touched by their warm atmosphere and dance with them.

3. Folk Art of Talking and Singing and Performance of Tibetan Opera

Folk songs, "Guoxie" and "Guozhuang" are spontaneous entertainment activities of Tibetan common people who participate in them. Two kinds of folk artistic activities are widely spread in

3.说唱曲艺和藏戏表演

歌谣、"果谐"和"锅庄"更多是藏人群众性自发的,大众参与的文娱活动。在藏区的民间还广泛流传着两种曲艺活动，体现了更高的艺术意趣，它们都是由专门的民间艺人来担当表演的，在藏区各大节日庆典和仪式活动上都是不可或缺的活动。一个是各种形式的说唱艺术，另外一个就是藏戏表演。虽然在艺术分类中，现在经常把说唱艺术和藏戏表演区分开来介绍，但实际上这两者有着不可分割的联系，不管是两种艺术的起源和发展或者是表演形式都是相互影响，我中有你，你中有我的。

说唱曲艺

所谓说唱曲艺，广义上来讲其实就是通过说说唱唱、似说似唱、吟诵说唱，既说又唱来讲故事的艺术。藏地是故事的海洋，藏族不管农牧区还是城镇群众都非常喜欢听优美的民间说唱故事，人们常常听故事，听得入迷了，有时甚至忘了一天繁重劳动后的疲劳，忘记吃饭睡觉。听唱故事不仅给

the Tibetan areas, they present high artistic charm, are performed by professional folk artists, and are indispensable activities on festival celebrations and cercmonies in the Tibetan areas. One is folk art of talking and singing in different forms, and the other is performance of Tibetan opera. As for the art categories, we introduce folk art of talking and singing and performance of Tibetan opera separately at present, but the two arts are linked with each other, they have mutual influence in terms of origin and development or performance forms, and they are inseparable.

Folk Art of Talking and Singing

As for folk art of talking and singing, it is the art of telling stories through talking, singing, semi-talking and semi-singing. The Tibetan areas are the ocean of stories. Common people in Tibetan agricultural and pastoral areas and towns like listening to beautiful folk rap stories very much. People often listen to ravishing stories, even forget fatigue after a day's heavy labor, dining or sleeping. Listening to rap stories can add infinite pleasure to their monotonous life, open the window to people's soul, and they can acquire knowledge through listening to stories. During festivals, people regard listening to rap stories as an entertainment activity which adds festival happiness. Rich families will invite folk artists who can tell rap stories to their houses to tell stories, it's very cheerful that all family members listen to stories with thirsty ears, and some storytellers will even tell stories for several nights consecutively.

In the Tibetan areas, there is no uniform concept of "folk art" actually, but names are called according to specific talking and singing varieties such as "Zhega", "Lamamani", "Lingzhong" and so on. In the Tibetan areas, folk art of talking and singing can be probably divided into "Zhong and Zhonglu", i.e. talking and singing stories; "Guerlu", i.e. speech song; "Xieba and Duiba", i.e. eulogy and good wishes; "Bai", i.e. expedition and morale-boosting songs of ancient soldiers; "Zhongling", i.e. Geshaer talking and singing; "Lamamani" is mainly used for talking and singing of religious ceremonies; "Zhega" is a kind of performance form of folk artists who come to houses to sing praises and perform stories on festivals; "Zhanian performance", i.e. chanting and playing with Zhanian instrument; and "Xia", i.e. singing songs

人们单调的生活增添了无限乐趣，还开启了人们心灵的窗户，对于一般百姓来说他们可以通过听故事学到很多原来自己不懂的东西。而在节庆期间，人们更是将听说唱故事作为一项娱乐活动，以增添节日的欢乐。家境比较富裕的人甚至专门请会讲唱故事的民间艺人到家里讲故事，一家人围在一起津津有味地听故事其乐融融，有些甚至一讲就是连续几个夜晚。

在藏区，其实并没有一个"曲艺"的统称概念，而是把诸如"折嘎"、"喇嘛玛呢"、"岭仲"等具体说唱品种直呼其名。在藏区，说唱曲艺大概可分为："仲和仲鲁"，即说唱故事；"古尔鲁"，即道歌；"谐巴和堆巴"，即赞词和祝颂；"百"，古代藏族士兵征战和壮威歌；"岭仲"，即格萨尔说唱；"喇嘛玛呢"主要是用于宗教仪式的说唱；"折嘎"，则是一种由民间艺人在节假喜庆之日登门唱赞颂、故事表演形式；"扎年弹唱"，即为弹着扎年琴的唱诵；"夏"，就是对唱歌谣以及藏语相声大概这十个类型[1]。

这几种类型虽然都是说唱曲艺，但是各有各的特点。对藏区的普通老百姓来说，通常在节日庆典间，譬如新年、婚庆、搬新房等最喜闻乐见的就是"谐巴堆巴"、"折嘎"还有藏语相声。"谐巴堆巴"是对各种东西的赞美之词，内容非常广泛，涉及达官贵人、活佛、高僧、长辈、亲朋好友、人间事理、人文景观、大自然、天文地理等，有单口和群口两类，除了有一定的固定唱段而外，说唱者一般都能即兴创作，所以它在老百姓日常生活当中运用很广泛。

另外就是"折嘎"，"折嘎"本意是指在每逢新年佳节和喜庆盛会之际上门祝福唱赞颂词的民间

in antiphonal style and Tibetan comic dialogue, and there are probably ten types[1].

Although these types can be classified into folk art of talking and singing, they have their own characteristics. As for Tibetan common people, what one would like to see and hear are "Xiebaduiba", "Zhega" and Tibetan comic dialogue during celebrations and festivals, such as, New Year, wedding celebration, moving into new houses etc. "Xiebaduiba" is complementing various kinds of thing. Its wide contents involve prominent officials and eminent personages, living Buddhas, eminent monks, the senior, relatives and good friends, folk ethic, humanistic landscapes, nature, astronomy and geography etc. It is divided into single and group, and rappers often improvise spontaneously except some certain sections, so it is widely applied in daily life of common people.

As for "Zhega", it originally meant folk artists who visit houses to bless and sing praise songs on occasions such as New Year, festivals, happy meetings. These "Zhega" artists were rather low

[1]参见《西藏百科全书》361页，西藏人民出版社2005年版。

[1]Refer to *Encyclopedia of Tibet*, p361, Tibet People's Publishing House, 2005.

in social position in the past, they often held five-colored sticks in hands, carried masks on shoulders, and carried big wooden bowls in clothes to perform as beggers in the entire Tibetan areas. However, Tibetan common people like these Zhega artists very much, call them the embodiment of good luck, and they also call themselves the representative of good luck.

In Lhasa, when a Zhega artist visits in the morning on the first day of the first month in the Tibetan calendar, he is regarded as an auspicious symbol, so the master and his family propose toasts and serve tea to him, offer money and articles, and present Hada to him. At this time, Zhega hails loudly, "Gegesuosuo, may good gods prevail!" He tries his best to praise heavenly gods, throws Zanba powder to the sky in order to sacrifice to gods. In order to make wishes for luck and perfection, he claim, "The stars shine in the sky, it is warm on the earth, and I wish you happiness and luck in good time today." Or he says the words such as "Wish you good luck and fortune" or other lucky words such as "Firstly, I congratulate you on climbing to the top of Snow Mountain, your heart is purer than snow, and I wish you purity and happiness. La! Secondly, I congratulate you on climbing to the top of rock. La! Wish you longevity like perpetual red rock in the world. Thirdly, I congratulate you on walking towards river, and wish you reproduction for generations like blue and everlasting rivers! La!

艺人。这些折嘎艺人过去的社会地位都比较低下，一般都是手持五色棍，肩背假面具，怀揣大木碗到全藏各地进行乞讨性的表演。但是藏族老百姓一般都非常喜欢这些折嘎艺人，称他们是吉祥的化身，折嘎艺人也称自己是吉祥的象征。

在拉萨，藏历大年初一早晨，当折嘎艺人登门来访，被视作吉祥的象征，主人家热情地向他敬酒敬茶，布施钱物，并向折嘎艺人献哈达。这时折嘎会大声欢呼："咯咯唆唆，愿善神得胜！"尽量说一些赞美天神的话，向苍天撒糌粑粉，以示敬祀天下神灵。同时为了表示对吉祥圆满的祝福，朗声："今日天星亮晶晶，今日地上暖洋洋，在今日美好良辰，祝你们美满吉祥。"或者说"祝福吉祥如意"之类的话；或者说些其他吉祥的说辞，如："首先，祝贺走上雪山巅，心脏比雪还洁白，白雪纯净永美满。啦！第二件喜事，祝贺登上岩石巅。啦！祝您寿比岩石长，红岩永恒儿世上。第三件喜事，祝您走向河中心，祈祝代代传优种，似碧波江河水流常。啦！哈哈！"专门说唱一些吉祥祝福词之后，折嘎就要进入正辞的说唱，先介绍折嘎的来历，它是怎样来的，为什么会出现这一曲种都要介绍一番；紧接着自我夸张，赞美折嘎自己的长相、服饰和道具的特殊作用，比如他的木棍、木碗和整个假面具。正辞说唱之后，再说些收场结尾的吉祥祝辞，如："啦！凡折嘎所到之处，漫天飘逸吉祥如意，凡折嘎所想所做，一定美满如愿以偿。天下喜事汇聚于我折嘎一身，折嘎向天地神灵、向喇嘛、向三宝祈祷！"

这些折嘎艺人虽然大都不识字，但是口齿伶俐，语言优美，见到什么就说唱什么，想到什么就说什么。表演形式生动活泼，说唱内容丰富，语言精练而极富渲染夸张，说到高兴处使人心花怒放，

Haw-haw!" After talking and singing some lucky benedictions, Zhega enters into the talking and singing of formal context, he introduces history of Zhega, how and why there is this kind of folk art; then he exaggerates himself, praises special roles of his appearance, clothes, ornaments and props, such as his wooden stick and bowl and the entire mask. After talking and singing the formal contexts, he says lucky words as epilogue, such as "La! Where Zhega comes, people have good luck and happiness; what Zhega desires will come true happily. Zhega represents all happy things under heaven, and it prays to gods in heaven and on earth, Lamas and Triratna!"

Although these Zhega artists are illiterate, they are clever and fluent, can sing for everything and talk about everything. Their performance forms are vivid, talking and singing contents are rich and diversified, language is explicit and exaggerated, people are highly delighted for exclamation, and are convulsed with laughter for fun. They enthusiastically eulogize for things deserving praises, and satirize things deserving criticism mercilessly. These talking rappers are always on the move, they can be seen and their talking and singing can be heard in any places in the Tibetan areas.

Besides folks, various kinds of modern prefectural and municipal art troupes and song and dance troupes absorb Zhega performance largely in the Tibetan areas. Apart from traditional lyrics, new Zhega works are developed, such as *Tibet Today, Luck and Happiness for Remote Honored Guests, Three-generation Zhega* which is a trio Zhega, *Auspicious Benedictions* which is a six-person Zhega and so on.

Besides these Tibetan traditional folk art performances, Tibetan comic dialogues are popular among common people in Tibet at present, and they often appear among entertainment performances on occasions of festivals and celebrations. Tibetan comic dialogue is a kind of new folk art variety which develops from integrating comic dialogues imported from Han people with Tibetan jokes with a long history and comic clown performance. It's said that Losangdorje inspected and learned from Hou Baolin's comic dialogues when he taught in Tibetan Department of Minzu University of China in Beijing, and he was attracted by Hou's artistic charms, studied on artistic performance rules and skill characteristics of Han people carefully in his

说到风趣处让人捧腹大笑。该赞颂的地方热情赞颂，该讽刺的地方也无情地讽刺。这些说唱艺人的流动性很大，在藏区的任何地方都能见到他们，听到他们的说唱。

现在在藏区，除了民间，各种现代的地市文工团、歌舞团也大量吸收折嘎表演，除了那些传统的唱词，还发展了很多新的折嘎作品。如《今日西藏》《远方的贵客吉祥如意》、三人折嘎《三代折嘎》、六人折嘎《吉祥的祝辞》等。

除了这些藏族传统的曲艺表演，在如今的西藏，藏语相声也颇受老百姓喜爱，也经常在他们节日庆典的娱乐表演中出现。藏语相声是自内地汉族引进的相声与藏族历史悠久的说笑话和传统喜剧丑角表演相融合而发展起来的一种新的曲艺品种。据说，洛桑多吉因之前在北京中央民族学院藏语系任教期间观摩了侯宝林说相声，深深被其艺术魅力所吸引，利用业余时间，潜心对汉族的相声艺术表演规律和技艺特点进行了学习研究。回到西藏之后，他借助藏语文内涵丰富的特点和藏族传统"谐巴"（即逗笑表演）表演的基础，融合内地相声艺术的特点，首先改编创作和表演了藏语相声《醉酒》，正式演出后获得了极大的成功。从此这一艺术形式不仅得到了藏族群众的接受和认可，同时也十分地受欢迎，在藏区得到了迅速地传播。在节日庆典的活动上，经常有藏语相声表演，电台、电视台也经常演播，总是能看到人们被逗笑得乐开了花的样子。一些著名的剧目有比如：《歌舞的海洋》《四不像》《出丑记》《尼玛教师回来了》《茶酒的风波》，等等。

spare time. After returning to Tibet, he integrated artistic characteristics of comic dialogue with performance conventions of Tibetan traditional "Xieba" (amusing performance) in the inner land on the basis of rich connotations of Tibetan Language, adapted, created and performed Tibetan comic dialogue *Drunkenness* firstly, and it made great success after being formally performed. From then on, this artistic form has been accepted and recognized by Tibetan common people, been very popular and quickly spread in the Tibetan areas. There are Tibetan comic dialogue performances in festival and celebration activities, which are performed and broadcast in radio stations and TV stations, and people are often amused greatly. There are some famous operas, such as *Ocean of Songs and Dances, Four Unlikeness, Becoming a Laughing Stock, Teacher Nima Comes Back, Disturbance of Tea Wine* and so on.

Tibetan Opera Performance

Tibetan opera performance is a program which is more outstanding during festival celebration in the Tibetan areas. It can be seen at various temple and folk ceremonies and activities. During each Tibetan New Year, people get together on squares, participate in all kinds of prayer ceremonies of temples. Wonderful Tibetan operas after religious ceremonies, which are amusing songs and dances performed by secular troupes, enliven festival atmosphere mainly, win joy of common people,

藏戏表演

在藏地节日庆典上，藏戏表演是一个更加引人瞩目的节目。从寺庙到民间的各种仪式和活动上都可以见到它的身影。每年藏历年间，人们汇聚广场，参加寺庙的各种法会仪式，在宗教仪式进行之后往往就有精彩的藏戏演出，藏戏演出特别是俗人戏班的演出多是歌舞谐笑之剧，主要活跃节日气氛，博得群众欢乐，深受藏地民众的喜爱，这也成为节日庆典时候各个仪式当中吸引人眼球的一大看点。

藏戏其实是一个非常庞大的剧种系统，是对藏族戏剧的泛称。但由于青藏高原各地自然条件、生活习俗、文化传统、方言语音的不同，藏戏实际上拥有众多的艺术品种和流派。这里由于篇幅所限，介绍的也只能是一般情况，难以将所有支派的藏戏一一涉及。

不过，关于藏戏的起源有个非常美丽的传说。在藏区，人们称藏戏为"拉姆"或"阿吉拉姆"，意为"仙女"或"仙女姐姐"。用这么优美而令人遐思的词来命名一门戏剧实在比较少见，这就跟它起源的传说非常有关。

传说，那个时候，雅鲁藏布江上没有什么桥梁，数不清的牛皮船，被掀翻在野马脱缰般的激流中，许多试图过江的百

take the fancy of Tibetans, and become an attracting watching focus among ceremonies during festival celebrations.

Actually, Tibetan opera is a very large opera genre system, and is the general term for Tibetan drama. Because of differences of natural conditions, customs, cultural tradition, dialect and pronunciation, Tibetan opera has diversified artistic varieties and genres. I only introduce general aspects here because of limited length of this book, and cannot talk about Tibetan operas in all genres.

However, the origin of Tibetan opera has a very beautiful legend. In the Tibetan areas, people call Tibetan opera "Lamu" or "Ajilamu", meaning "fairy" or "fairy sister". It's rare to use such a beautiful and thought-provoking name to call a drama, and it is related to its original legend.

It was said that there were no bridges on Yarlung Zangbo River, numerous bull boats were thrown in the unbridled torrent, and many common people who tried to cross rivers were swallowed by howling water. Therefore, a young monk named

Tongdong Gyibo made a grand wish, and vowed to build bridges and bring benefits to people. However, Tongdong Gyibo who was a nobody caused a storm of laughter.

Hereafter, Tongdong Gyibo got acquainted with seven girls who were good at songs and dances in Shannan Qiongjie, formed the first Tibetan opera troupe, then adopted the form of singing, dancing and talking to perform religious stories and historical legends, persuade people to do good things and accumulate merits, contribute money and labor to build bridges commonly. Hearing powerful songs reverberated in Snow Mountains and open fields, some people contributed money, some people offered ingots, some people sent provisions, and a large quantity of peasants and artisans followed them to walk from one bridging site to another bridging site...

The seeds of Tibetan opera were sowed in snow region plateau. People praised girls' beautiful appearance, charming gestures, graceful and fresh voices and claimed that "Ajilamus descend to the world and dance!" Hereafter, people called Tibetan opera performance "Ajilamu". In this way, penniless Tongdong Gyibo crented fifty-eight chain bridges on Yarlung zangbo River, and became the earliest founder of Tibetan opera.[1]

---

[1]Refer to baike.baidu.com: Tibetan Opera, http://baike.baidu.com/view/74674.htm.

姓，被咆哮的江水吞噬。于是，一个年轻的僧人唐东杰布许下宏愿，发誓架桥，为民造福。但是一无所有的唐东杰布，招来的只是一阵哄堂大笑。

可是，后来唐东杰布在山南琼结结识能歌善舞的七位姑娘，组成了西藏的第一个藏戏班子，用歌舞说唱的形式，表演宗教故事、历史传说，劝人行善积德、出钱出力、共同修桥。随着雄浑的歌声响彻雪山旷野，有人献出钱财，有人布施铁块，有人送来粮食，更有大批的农民、工匠跟着他们，从一个架桥工地，走到另一个架桥工地……

藏戏的种子随之撒遍了雪域高原。所到之处，人们为姑娘们美丽的容貌、婀娜的舞姿、优美清新的唱腔赞叹不已，观众惊叹道："莫不是阿吉拉姆下凡跳舞了吧！"以后人们就将藏戏演出称为"阿吉拉姆"。就这样，身无分文的唐东杰布在雅鲁藏布江上留下了58座铁索桥，同时，成为藏戏的开山鼻祖。①

所以，现在在每场藏戏演出的时候都会看到演员将唐东杰布的像供奉在戏场上。

藏戏的演出，一般是广场戏，少数有舞台演出的形式，选比较平旷的场子，画一圆周，栏以绳柱，缺一块地方为演员出入之路。场的正中，插一株白杨，下设短桌，供演剧之神——唐东杰布。其余的空地就是演剧的地方。观看的人就环立在圆圈外，很像马戏场。吹打乐器的就坐在剧场边际。

藏戏演出的乐器比较简单，打击乐只有一鼓一钹，演员化妆也比较简单，除了戴面具外，其他就只是一般的粉面与红脂，没有复杂的脸谱。演出的时候有一人在旁用快板向观众介绍剧情发展的情况，这跟其他的戏剧演出相比比较特别，剧情介绍和演员的演唱在演出期间相间出现，还有一人通

①参见百度百科：藏戏，http://baike.baidu.com/view/74674.htm。

Therefore, actors offer the image of Tongdong Gyibo in theatre when each Tibetan opera is performed at present.

As for performance of Tibetan opera, usually square operas are performed and only a few operas adopt the form of stage performance. Flat and open field is selected, a circle is fenced with ropes and posts, and a space is left for entry and exit of actors. A white poplar is inserted in the middle of the scene, and a short table is put under it to sacrifice to Tongdong Gyibo, who is thought to be the god of opera performance. The rest open space is the place for opera performance. The audience stand outside the circle, which looks like a circus. Instrument players sit at the edge of the theatre.

Instruments for Tibetan opera are very simple, and there are only a drum and a cymbal for percussion music. Actors dress up simply, and they usually wear masks as well as pink powder and rouge, rather than complicated masks. During the performance, one person introduces the plot development to the audience with clappers, which differs from performance of other operas, plot introductions and singing of actors appear alternatively, and one person usually joins in talking and singing behind the stage. Differing from folk art of talking and singing, Tibetan opera focuses on singing, persons seldom speak in opera, and actors often sing loudly and clearly with a lot of long and drawn-out tunes because of the size of square, which show their bold and powerful personality. Tibetan opera has many tunes including long tune representing happiness, which is called "Dangren" in Tibetan, sad tune representing suffering and gloom, which is called "Danglu" in Tibetan, short tune representing narration, which is called "Dangtong" and so on[1].

Performance of Tibetan opera can usually be divided into three parts: the opening ceremony "Aruowa", the formal performance "Xiong" and the auspicious closing ceremony "Tashi". The opening ceremony can also be called "Wenbadun" or "Jialu Wenba", and the contents mainly include site cleaning sacrifice, praying to gods and dispelling evils, praying for blesses, and introducing plots. Usually, characters appearing on the scene include two Jialus, seven Wenbas and seven Lamus. It's said that these three types of characters are evolved from the characters in *Qujie Lobsang*. Jialu is a prince, Wenba is a fisherman or hunter, and Lamu is a fairy. During the performance, Wenbas sing and jump with masks, then Lumus lead a group of fairies to sing and dance, introduce actors and explain plot of

常在后台帮腔、和唱。与说唱艺术不太相同的是藏戏是以唱为主，剧中人道白很少，由于通常是广场演出，演员的唱腔多高昂嘹亮，拖腔也比较多，显示出粗犷有力的性格。藏戏的唱腔也有很多，大致分为表现欢乐的长调，藏语叫"党仁"；表现痛苦忧愁的悲调，藏语称"党鲁"；表现叙述的短调，藏语称"党统"，等等[1]。

藏戏的演出一般都分为三个部分：开场仪式"阿若娃"、正戏"雄"和吉祥收尾仪式"扎西"。开场仪式又称为"温巴顿"或"甲鲁温巴"，其内容主要是净场祭祀，祈神驱邪，祈求祝福，并介绍剧情。出场人物一般有：甲鲁二人、温巴七人、拉姆七人。传说这三种人物是根据《曲结洛桑》剧中人物演变而来。甲鲁是王子，温巴是渔夫或猎人，拉姆是仙女。表演时先是温巴戴着

①Refer to baike.baidu.com: Tibetan Opera, http://baike.baidu.com/view/74674.htm.

①参见百度百科：藏戏，http://baike.baidu.com/view/74674.htm。

面具又唱又跳，然后甲鲁领着一群仙女出场歌舞，借以介绍演员，讲解正戏的剧情，招揽观众。"雄"是正戏，先由"温巴格更"（即戏师）用快板韵白介绍故事情节、地点、环境、人物造型、唱词等，然后人物上场。演出时间长则三天三夜，甚至六七天；短则两三小时，皆由戏师控制决定。其表演形式为：全体演员，不论是否扮演剧中角色，全部出场，围成半圈，然后由一个角色出来演唱一段，然后所有演员共同起舞或表演技巧，彼此循环。其演出不分幕和场次，剧情讲解者和伴唱伴舞实际上起着分幕的作用。由于传统剧目一般都是流传上百年，甚至几百年的经典之作，所以大多数观众都熟悉戏中的人物和故事情节。他们观看演出主要是欣赏剧中唱腔、舞蹈和特技等。因情节发展由戏师介绍，剧中人物可专心演唱或表演绝技。通过戏师巧妙安排，一台故事动人、唱腔优美、

formal performance to attract the audience. "Xiong" is formal performance, and "Wenba Gegeng" (i.e. opera master) introduces plot, place, environment, character profiles, and words of songs with clappers rhythmically, then the actors appear on the scene. The performance time lasts three days and three nights, even six or seven days; or it lasts only two or three hours, which is controlled and decided by opera master. The performance form is that all actors appear on the scene in a semicircle, no matter what roles are played, one role comes out to sing a section, then all actors dance commonly or perform skills, and they perform in cycles one another. The performance has no acts and scenes, plot interpreter and vocal and dance accompaniments play the role of act division. Traditional programs have been passed down for several hundred years, and they have been classical works for several hundred years, so most of audiences are familiar with characters and plots in plays. They watch performance to appreciate tunes, dances and stunts etc. in plays. Because plot development is introduced by opera master, characters in play can sing or perform stunts carefully. Through delicate arrangement of opera master, a wonderful artistic form with beautiful story, graceful tunes, attractive stunts, vocal and dance accompaniments of actors on the scene is presented to the audience. "Tashi" is collective singing and dancing at the end of Tibetan opera performance, which means best wishes and good luck.

特技表演扣人心弦，并有
同台演员帮腔伴舞的精美
艺术形式就展现在观众面
前。"扎西"是藏剧演出
结尾时的集体歌舞，意为
祝福吉祥。

Differing from folk art of talking and singing, Tibetan opera is a life-style performance focusing on singing and integrating basic procedures such as singing, reciting, dancing, performance, aside, skills and so on. Martial art, dance and various kinds of artistic skills are widely applied into Tibetan opera performance. Usually, there is a dance after a song. There are many dancing acts, such as climbing mountain, sailing, flying in the sky, diving into the sea, riding horses, fighting with devils, catching monsters, worshiping Buddhas and so on, and they have certain gestures. Therefore, its performance is one of important factors to attract the audience.

与说唱艺术不太相
同，藏戏是以唱为主，集
唱、诵、舞、表、白和技
等基本程式为一体的生
活化的表演。武功、舞
蹈、各种技艺在藏戏演出
中，也广泛运用。一般是
演唱一段以后，便出现
一段舞蹈。舞蹈动作很
多，爬山、行船、飞天、
入海、骑马、斗妖、擒
魔、礼佛等，都有一定
的舞姿。所以，它的极
具表演性也是吸引观众
的一大重要因素。

Program of Tibetan opera performance can be divided into two types, i.e. traditional program of Tibetan opera and modern program of Tibetan opera. Its traditional programs include *Princess Wencheng* and *Children in Reqiong* which are the historical legend plays; *Prince Lobsang* which is the mythic love play; *Suji Nima* and *Genquebo* which are the plays of myth and legend; *Baima Wenba*, which is the child hero play, *Langsa Wenbang* which is the social life play taken from realistic materials; *Zhuowa Sangmu, Dunyue Dunzhu, Dide Gede* and

藏戏演出的剧目分为
传统藏戏剧目和现代藏戏
剧目两大类。它的传统剧
目有：历史传说剧《文成
公主》和《热琼娃》；民
间故事改编的神话爱情戏
《诺桑王子》；神话传说
剧《苏吉尼玛》和《根却
波》；儿童英雄剧《白玛
文巴》；直接取材于现实
材料的社会生活剧《朗萨

雯蚌》；人情世态剧《卓娃桑姆》《顿月顿珠》《敌得格得》和《曲吉朗桑》；宗教故事剧《智美更登》《云乘王子》《德巴登巴》《絮巴旺秋》和《敬巴钦保》；还有藏族古典小说改编的《郑宛达娃》等。现在在藏区民间普遍流传的有八大传统剧目《文成公主》《诺桑王子》《卓娃桑姆》《朗萨雯蚌》《白玛文巴》《顿月顿珠》《智美更登》和《苏吉尼玛》。在1959年西藏民主改革后，西藏藏剧团还创作了一系列中小型现代藏戏[1]。

在藏戏演出中，最有特色的是它的面具和服饰。藏语称面具为"巴"，是藏戏独有的面部化妆手段。据说藏戏的面具最初主要来自于宗教哑剧舞蹈仪式——羌姆，后来藏戏表演者按藏戏始祖唐东杰布面目制作了白发白须的白山羊皮面具。在之后的发展当中，藏戏

Quji Langsang which are the secular world plays; *Zhimei Gengdeng, Prince Yuncheng, Deba Dengba, Xuba Wangqiu* and *Jingba Qinbao* which are the religious story plays; *Zhengwan Dawa* which is adapted from the Tibetan classical novel and so on. There are eight traditional folk programs which are popular in Tibet, including *Princess Wencheng, Prince Lobsang, Zhuowa Sangmu, Langsa Wenbang, Baima Wenba, Dunyue Dunzhu, Zhimei Gengdeng* and *Suji Nima*. After Tibet's Democratic Reform in 1959, Tibetan Opera Troupe has created a series of small and medium-sized modern Tibetan plays[1].

In Tibetan opera performance, the most striking characteristics are its masks and clothes. Mask is called as "Ba" in Tibetan and is the unique facial make-up measure of Tibetan opera. It's said that masks of Tibetan opera originally were from Qiangmu, which was the religious pantomime dance ceremony, and Tibetan opera performers made white goatskin masks with white hair and beard according to appearance of Tangdong Gyibo, the founder of the Tibetan opera. During the latter development, Tibetan opera masks have developed into more

---

[1]参见《藏族百科全书》，491—492页，西藏人民出版社 2005年版。

[1]Refer to *Encyclopedia of Tibet*, pp491-492, Tibet People's Publishing House, 2005.

types, they have uniqueness, i.e., dark red mask represents king, light red mask represents minister, yellow mask represents living Buddha, blue mask represents hunter, green mask represents woman, white mask represents man, black mask represents negative character, semi-white and semi-black mask represent double-dealer in Tibetan opera and so on. Tibetan opera mask can be divided into Wenba mask, character mask and animal mask. As for Wenba mask, Wenba means "fisherman or hunter" in Tibetan, and these marks can be divided into white and blue types. As for character mask, many types exist, and there are two forms mainly, i.e. two-dimension and three-dimension. Two-dimension masks are made of various kinds of cloths, paper plates and goatskin etc., and represent roles with identity and personality, such as characters in real life including king, minister, Lama, old woman, old man, witch and so on; three-dimension masks are made of paper pulp, wax cloth, and mud etc., and they represent fairies and monsters in opera, such as Maitreya, dragon daughter, Yama Dharmapala and Azharang making impromptu comic gestures and remarks, and also animals in various kinds of forms. Masks in different colors represent different characters with different artistic and exaggerated colorful styles, such as blue Wenba mask symbolizes courage and justice, red mask worn by king symbolizes power, yellow mask worn by minister symbolizes loyalty, green mask worn by princess and herdswoman symbolizes femininity, white mask worn by good man symbolizes kindness,

面具发展出更多的种类，藏戏面具十分独特，在藏戏中，深红色面具代表国王，浅红色面具代表大臣，黄色面具代表活佛，蓝色面具代表猎人，绿色面具代表女性，白色面具代表普通男性，黑色面具代表反面人物，半白、半黑面具代表两面派，等等。藏戏面具分为温巴面具、人物面具和动物面具。温巴面具，温巴，藏语的意思就是"渔夫或猎人"，面具又分白、蓝两类；人物面具，种类较多，主要有平面和立体两种形式。平面面具用各种布料、纸板、山羊皮等组合而成，多用来表现剧中有身份、有性格的角色，如国王、大臣、喇嘛以及老妇、老翁、巫女等现实生活中的人物；立体面具用纸浆、漆布、泥巴等塑成，立体面具除有各种造型的动物外，还有表现剧中的神仙鬼怪，如弥勒佛、龙女、阎罗王护法神以及插科打诨的角色阿扎让等。各种颜色的面具以艺术夸张的色彩表现各种

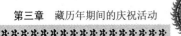
人物的不同性格，如剧中的蓝温巴面具是勇敢和正义的象征，国王戴的红面具则是权力的象征，忠臣戴的黄色面具象征忠良，王妃、牧女戴绿面具象征女性，良家老人戴的白面具象征善良，口是心非、两面三刀的角色戴的是半白、半黑的面具，而黑色面具则表现凶恶与残暴；动物面具，在藏戏中，无论什么流派和剧种都离不开各种动物的登台表演。因此，藏戏中有众多的动物面具。这些动物都被罩上神灵的色彩，实际上是一种图腾崇拜。如西藏原始苯教所崇拜的神祇是羊头、牛头、马头和虎头，这些动物的面具代表着各种有生命的神灵。

藏戏服饰丰富多彩，具有鲜明的民族风格和高原雪域特色。蓝面具戏的藏戏服饰具有藏族的肥腰、长袖、大襟、袒臂的特点，色彩艳丽浓重，注重纹样结构组合，喜用兽皮、金银、珠宝、象牙、宝石等作为饰物。同时，腰带又是佩挂装饰品

double-faced role wears semi-white and semi-black mask, and black mask symbolizes fierceness and cruelty. As for animal masks, different schools and genres of drama cannot separate from stage performance of various kinds of animals in Tibetan opera. Therefore, there are numerous animal masks in Tibetan opera. These animals have the celestial color, which is a kind of totem worship in fact. For example, gods worshiped by Tibetan Bonism are sheep, ox, horse and tiger heads, and masks of these animals represent deities of life.

Tibetan opera clothes are rich and colorful, and have the distinctive ethnic styles, plateau and snowland features. Tibetan opera clothes and ornaments in blue mask are characterized by fat waist, long sleeve, wide collar and naked arm of Tibetans, colors are bright and heavy, attention is paid to combination of pattern structure, and hides, gold, silver, pearls, jewels, elephant's tusk, gemstones etc. are used as ornaments. Meanwhile, waistband is the main part of hanging ornament, waist ornaments with pearls and jewels in various styles are tied on waist and hung down over hips, and constitute various kinds of tail decorations. These clothes and ornaments are mainly based on Tibetan clothes and ornaments from the ancient Tubo period, and develop through historical evolvement and absorption of Mongolian clothes and ornaments of the Yuan Dynasty and forms of official clothes of the Qing Dynasty. Usually, leaders of folk troupes or temples are responsible for making Tibetan opera clothes, and a few aristocrats, officials and great monks in temples raise funds to make them for folk troupes, and villagers and monks in some villages, towns and temple troupes offer materials and raise funds for some villages, towns and temple troupes. After Tibet's Democratic Reform, the making of opera clothes adopts the latter method basically. Tibetan opera clothes include clothes of kings, ministers, attendants, servants, Lamas, nuns, Jialus, Wenbas, Lamus, dancing gods and fair ladies.

Besides Tibetan New Year and other festival celebrations, the annual Shoton Festival can represent that Tibetans attach importance to Tibetan opera and are keen on it. It has another name, i.e. Tibetan Opera Festival. On the first day of the seventh month in Tibetan calendar, residents from various parts of Tibet including Lhasa come to Luobu Kalin to watch united performance of

的主要部位，各种式样镶有珠宝的腰佩系在腰上，垂在臀部，构成各式各样的尾饰。这些服饰主要以古代吐蕃时期藏族服饰为基础，后经历史演变，吸收元朝蒙古族服饰和清代官服的形制样式发展而成。藏戏服装的制作一般都由民间戏班所属之领主头人或所依靠的寺院负责置办，也有少数贵族、官员和寺院高僧为民间戏班出资置办，还有部分村镇和寺院戏班由村民及僧众捐献物资钱款集体置办。在西藏民主改革之后，基本就是以后一种方式来置办戏服。藏戏服饰主要有：国王服、大臣服、侍从佣人服；喇嘛服、尼姑服、甲鲁服、温巴服、拉姆服、跳神服和贵夫人服几种。

除了藏历新年和其他的一些节日庆典，最能够体现藏人对藏戏的重视和喜爱的就是每年的雪顿节。雪顿节还有另外一个名字即为藏戏节，在这一天，也即藏历七月初一的那一天，拉萨等西藏各地的居民来到罗布卡林，观看来自拉萨、日喀则、琼结、雅砻、堆龙德庆等地的藏戏团和藏戏班子、舞班子、打鼓舞队的联合演出。初八以后，各剧团到拉萨地区各处演出，八月上旬各剧团回到本地。同时，全藏区村寨所有民间藏戏团体和带有戏剧性质的艺术表演团队，和僧俗一起狂欢。因此雪顿节又可以说是一个藏戏的狂欢节日。

Tibetan opera troupes and groups, dance groups, drum and dance teams from Lhasa, Shigatse, Qonggyai, Yarlung, Doilungdeqen and so on. Since the eighth day, the troupes perform all over Lhasa, and they come back in early August. Meanwhile, all folk Tibetan opera bodies and artistic performance groups in the nature of drama revel with monks all over the Tibetan areas. Therefore, Shoton Festival can be seen as a carnival of Tibetan opera.

4. Sports and Athletic Activities: Wrestling, Carrying Stone and Casting Stone

After a series of grand ceremonial performances, celebration activities are not complete in Tibet during New Year, and the noisiest folk recreational and athletic activities begin. Usually, the first program held on Lhasa Barkhor Square is wrestling. Tibetan wrestling is called "Beiga", and its form is similar to modern judo somewhat. During the competition, both parties wear Tibetan gowns with broad waist band, and they hold waists each other. Referee declares the starting and stopping. When wrestling, one participant shall throw his opponent to the ground with power of hands and waist, and using legs breaks the rules. Except legs, falling of any parts of body on the ground is regarded as being defeated. Sometimes, there is no list of sportsmen, neither is roll call nor announcement before competition, and it starts when a piece of mat is laid on the ground, winner and loser receive the same honor and prizes.

Besides wrestling, there is a kind of old competition in the Tibetan areas, which is called competition of carrying stone. It may be one of the oldest and the most primitive entertainment forms as well as wrestling, it has been popular for generations and

四、体育竞技活动——摔跤、抱石、掷石

新年期间的西藏，当一系列隆重的仪式表演过去以后，庆祝活动并没有结束，真正最热闹的一系列民间娱乐竞技活动才拉开帷幕。通常在拉萨八廓街广场上第一个开始的项目就是摔跤。藏式摔跤称"北嘎"，其形式有点接近现代的柔道。比赛时，双方身着藏袍，系宽腰带，各自搂住对方腰部。由仲裁人宣布起止。在摔搏的时候，只准用手和腰部力量将对方摔倒，用腿则算犯规。除了腿之外，身体的任何部位着地都被认为是输了。比赛有些时候没有运动员的名单，也没有比赛前的点名与通告，有时一块毡片往地上一铺，比赛就开始了，胜者与败者受同样的荣誉和奖品。

除了摔跤，藏区还有一种很古老的比赛，抱石比赛。它和摔跤一样可能是藏族最古老、最原始的娱乐形式之一，富有群众基础和力量以及技巧性。历史上有举石碑、举石鼎一类的赛事。竞赛所抱石头，为圆形，重约150公斤，比赛时在石头上遍抹酥油，以增加难度。赛手躬腰抓握石头，托到双腿上，再挺身把石头举升到肩膀上，要求身直而不能晃动，然后再将石头稳稳地放回地面，即为成功。有的则双手拖石，绕场一周。以所抱石头的重量和时间的长短判别优胜者。

接着还有掷石比赛。掷石，是一种民间消遣，多为年轻人所为。一般是树立目标，然后参加者站在离目标百米远的地方，轮流对着目标用臂掷石，比赛力量与准确性。这种娱乐方式，在田间野外均可进行，不受条件限制。另一种为"古朵"，即用羊毛编织的牧鞭抛掷石头。"古朵"原为狩猎和放牧的工具。在藏族古代，它是一种武器，曾用来狠狠打击过入侵者。"古朵"呈带形，长约1.5米，两端细，一端有圈套；中间有一宽约4厘米的

involves power and skills. There were events such as lifting stone tablets and cauldrons in history. The stone for the competition is round, its weight is about 150kg, and in order to increase difficulties, it is smeared with ghee when the competition starts. The participant bows to grasp the stone, holds it to both legs, and straightens his back to lift to his shoulders, his body shall keep straight and shall not shake, then he puts it back on the ground, and he makes it. Some participants pull stones with both hands and walk around a circle. Weight of stone and duration are used to judge winner.

There is competition of casting stone next. Casting stone is a kind of folk entertainment of young people. The target is erected usually, then participants stand at the place one hundred meters away from the target, they cast stones in turn and compete for strength and accuracy. This entertainment can be held in fields, and isn't limited by conditions. Another competition is "Guduo", which means casting stone with stock whip woven with wool. "Guduo" was the tool for hunting and grazing. In ancient Tibet, it was a weapon, and was used to hit invaders. It is strip-shaped, its length is about 1.5 meters, two ends are narrow, and one end has a snare; and there is an elliptic "Wuti" with the width of 4 centimeters in the middle, which is used to pack the stone. During the competition, participants stand in a row, Guduo is folded in half with a stone; then they tie the end with the snare on middle finger or ring finger, hold the other end with thumb and index finger, rotate it evenly into curve, aim at the target at the maximum speed, release thumb and index finger suddenly, cast the stone in an arc, and winner is determined by distance and alignment. Because herdsmen often use it, they can hit targets accurately, and even hit horns of running sheep. Guduo with embroidered nine-eye pattern is precious, and girls in pastoral areas use it as a gift for lovers.

Horse Racing

In Lhasa, several thousand of Lhasa residents and suburb peasants get together on Lhasa race ground on the third day of the first month in the Tibetan calendar every year and watch yearly racing performance. Horse racing is one of the most favorite athletic entertainments of Tibetans in seasons, festivals and on the occasions of feasts and parties of relatives and friends. It is the most popular sports in the Tibetan areas. Horse racing meetings are held all over Lhasa, and there are many types of horse racing, such as running horse, walking horse,

椭圆"乌梯"，用以包裹石头。比赛时，选手们站成一线，将"古朵"对折，中包石子；然后将有圈套的一端套在右手中指或无名指上，另一端用拇指和食指抓住，在身旁均匀挥转成弧形，当转至最高速度时，即对准目标，猛将拇指、食指放开，石子即呈弧形飞掷出去，以抛远、中的决胜负。因为牧民们经常使用它，所以一般都很准确，甚至能击中飞奔中的羊的犄角。"古朵"以绣有九眼花纹者为珍品，牧区姑娘们常以此作为赠送情人的礼物。

赛马

在拉萨，每年藏历大年初三，拉萨市民和市郊农民群众数千人，汇聚在拉萨赛马场，观看一年一度的赛马表演。赛马是藏人在岁时节令、亲友宴集的时候最喜爱的竞技娱乐之一。它也是藏区最普及的运动，除了拉萨各地均有赛马会，赛马的种类有许多，有跑马、走马、马上射击、马上抬哈达、马上杂技等。

若忽然听到从远处传来一阵急促的马蹄声，就知道是赛马开始了。最先进行的是跑马，跑马是比赛速度的，赛程有两三公里的短跑，也有十里左右的长跑。一般都有一个起点和终点，在拉萨常常是以哲蚌寺下的琼热苏山脚为起点，终点是拉萨附近的工布塘。赛马比速度，竞争比较激烈，参赛的马匹也比较多，骑手大多为年轻人和十几岁的少年。牧区赛马多无鞍子。比赛时，人们将马头马尾挽上五色彩绸，精心打扮。骑手们身着盛装，威风凛凛。以先到达终点者为胜。

走马不但讲速度，还要看马的走势步伐，好的走马不但速度快，步伐也非常平稳。比赛走马的骑手往往是善于策马、精于骑术的成年人。走马比赛均备鞍子，而且在马头、马尾和鞍子上披有五色彩带，马脖子上挂有铜铃。走马赛的距离一般

shooting on horse, carrying Hada on horse, and acrobatics on horse etc.

Rapid hoofs are heard from a distance suddenly, and it's time to begin horse racing. Firstly, running horse is held for speed competition, short racing distance is about two or three kilometers, and long racing distance is about ten kilometers. Usually, there are a starting point and an ending point, the starting point is Qiongresu Mountain under the Drepung Temple, and the ending point is Gongbo Pool near Lhasa. Horse racing competes for speed, and the competition is violent. There are many racing horses, and most horsemen are young men or teenagers. Most of racing horses in pastoral area have no saddles. During horse racing, people decorate horses with colored silk delicately. Riders wear splendid attires with great dignity. The person reaches the finishing point first is the winner.

Walking horse specializes in speed and walking stance and paces. Good walking horse has fast speed as well as smooth pace. Horsemen taking part in walking horse are adults who are good at riding horses and equestrian skills. Saddles are used for walking horse competition, colored ribbons are decorated on heads, tails and saddles of horses, and brass bells are tied around necks of horses. Distance of walking horse competition isn't long usually.

Picking Hada on horse is a sport competing for skills on horse. Firstly, a piece of Hada is put on the tract every few meters, and horsemen bend over to pick up Hadas on the ground when riding horse quickly. This sport requires that horsemen are quick of eye and deft of hand, and excellent contestants can pick up over ten Hadas in a round. Some places have stricter requirements, and horsemen pick up silk flowers and cigarette cases etc. rather than Hadas, which is more difficult.

Shooting on horse includes archery and rifle shooting on horse. Archery on horse means that a target is erected at certain distance in the center, when a horseman runs near the target, he takes a bow, draws an arrow to shoot the target quickly, he will be the winner if he hits the bull's eye. This is also the case for rifle shooting, and a person will be a winner if he shoots the bull's eye. The two sports can be combined into one, that is to say, a horseman carries bow, arrow and rifle, and two targets are erected, he takes the rifle to shoot the target firstly and then takes a bow and arrow to shoot the target when riding quickly. This sport requires that contestants shall be nimble and fast.

Toasting on flying horses are composed of three horsemen, the first horseman holds an empty cup and puts the cup on the track when riding a horse quickly, the second horseman holds a wine pot and pour wine into the cup when riding a horse quickly, and the third horseman picks up the cup with wine

不太长。

马上拾哈达，是一项比赛马上技巧的运动。先在跑道上每隔数米放一条哈达，骑手们在乘马飞驰中俯身捡起地上的哈达。这项运动要求骑手手疾眼快，优秀的选手跑一趟能拾起十多条哈达。有些地方要求更严，不是拾哈达，而是拾绢花、烟盒等，其难度更大。

马上射击，包括马上射箭、打靶等。马上射箭是在中央的一定距离外支一靶子，当乘马跑近靶子时，迅速取弓搭箭射向靶子，以射中靶心者为胜。以枪打靶也是如此，以打中靶心者为胜。这项运动有时合并为一项，即骑手背弓箭和枪，设两个靶，在乘马飞驰中，先取枪射靶，再取弓搭箭射靶。这项运动要求选手身手灵活快捷。

飞马敬酒由3名骑手组成，第一个骑手手举一空杯，在乘骑飞奔中将酒杯放在跑道边上，第二骑手手拿酒壶，同样在乘马飞驰中将酒斟入酒杯，第三个骑手在乘马飞奔中将有酒的杯子从地上端起，然后把酒敬给尊贵的客人。

马上运动惊险激烈，是藏区人最喜欢的运动。每次举行赛马活动，得胜者均有奖励，得奖者不但是本乡本土的英雄，也是家族的骄傲，人们都要为之庆贺。

when riding quickly and presents the wine to guests.

Sports on horse are thrilling and violent and are the favorite sports of Tibetans. Winners are awarded with prizes in each horse racing activity, and they are native heroes and family heroes, and people will congratulate them.

Shooting Howling Arrow

Shooting howling arrow is a favorite activity of Tibetans during festivals. It is held with horse racing, but this kind of arrow has special characteristics, and is called howling arrow. The arrowhead is diamond-shaped with four eyes, and it makes a noise when it is shot, therefore it is named. Howling arrow is divided into two types, one is competing for distance, and the other is competing for accuracy. As for competing for accuracy, a target with inner and outer rings is erected at first and a person who shoots more inner rings is a winner. In the past, shooting howling arrow was the favorite activity of Tibetan noble officials. Archery contest is held in Lalu Lawn on the third day of Tibetan New Year in Lhasa annually, and it is called "Cisong Langda", which means "heavenly arrow on the third day". At present, this kind of archery contest has become a popular athletic activity all over the Tibetan areas.

射响箭

射响箭，也是藏人在节日期间喜爱的一项活动。通常和赛马安排在一起进行，只是这种箭是一种相当有特色的箭，称为响箭。这种箭箭头为菱形，上有四个眼，箭射出去后发出呜呜的响声，故而得名。响箭比赛有两种，一种是比远，一种是比准。比准时，先支一箭靶，箭靶有内外环，以射中内环多者为胜。在过去，射响箭是西藏贵族官员非常喜爱的活动，在藏历年每年的初三就会在拉萨的拉鲁草场举行射箭比赛，射箭大赛叫"次松郎达"，意思是"初三天箭"。如今这种射箭比赛已经成为流行于藏地各个地区的一项竞技活动。

五、投骰子

除了一系列的娱乐竞技项目，藏族民间还流行许多有意思的娱乐游戏。在亲朋团聚的节日期间，这些游戏更给人们增添了不少欢乐。

藏语叫"晓纠"的，汉语为投骰子、掷骰子的意思。这是在藏族民间最为普及的一种娱乐游戏。但是这种娱乐活动，在过去，僧俗贵族和达官贵人是不屑一顾玩的，认为它太粗俗、太闹腾，有失身份。但是在西藏的民间，特别是比较底层的人群当中却一直十分流行。在夏日的林卡里，或者就是在街边，田间地头的休息当，常常看到投骰子的人三五成群；节日期间，亲朋团聚，三五个人围成一堆，以投骰子为乐，再加上几个围观助阵的人，一家人在一起全神贯注，热闹非凡。

虽然投骰子看上去只是一个大众的玩乐游戏，但是若仔细观察，会发现投骰子中的学问非常多，

5. Casting Dice

Besides a series of recreational and athletic events, there are many popular and interesting entertainment games among Tibetans. During festivals, relatives and friends get together, and these games add much happiness to them.

"Xiaojiu" in Tibetan means casting dice and throwing dice in Chinese. This is a popular game among Tibetans. However, clerical and secular aristocrats, high officials and noble lords scorned to play it, thought it was too vulgar, noisy and degrading. It has been popular among Tibetans, especially among people in lower classes. Groups of people often cast dice in forests, streets or fields in summer. During festivals, relatives and friends get together, three or five of them sit around to cast dice for fun, several persons watch them playing, and the whole family concentrate their attention on it, shout and wrangle lively.

Although casting dice looks like a popular play game, through careful observation, you will find that casting dice is a great and delicate knowledge, especially chanting words during casting dice include history, religion, characters and folk custom, and is a hard-won folk literature wealth.

The following devices must be prepared for casting dice: the first is a pair of dice, which is called "Xiao" in Tibetan; the second is a wooden bowl shaking dice, which is called "Xiaopao"; the third is a piece of round cushion, which is called "Xiaodian"; the fourth is one hundred and eight public chips, some people use shells, some people use broad beans, some people use match sticks etc.; the fifth is persons casting dice, each person shall have nine personal chips with individual unique symbols. These chips can be copper coins, colored wooden sticks, and plastic sheets etc.; in brief, chips of everyone cannot be identical. These devices are placed on square Tibetan table or cushion, and public chips are placed on it in the shape of crescent. Persons casting dice sit around Tibetan table or cushion, one person can play on his/her own, and two persons can be a team.

The game of casting dice can be divided into several steps probably. Firstly, every player of the game puts the dice into the wooden bowl in turn at the very beginning, mutters incantations, shakes it

非常精妙，特别是投骰子时候念诵的骰子词，其中历史、宗教、人物、民俗内容无所不包，是一笔难得的民间文学财富。

玩骰子必须准备以下几种器具：一是一副骰子，藏语叫做"晓"；二是一个摇骰子的木碗，藏语叫做"晓抛"；三是一块圆形的皮垫子，藏语叫"晓垫"；四是一百零八颗公共筹码，有些是用贝壳，有些是用蚕豆，有些用火柴棍，等等；五是玩骰子的人，每个人必须有九个具有本人独特标志的个人筹码。这些筹码可以是铜钱，可以是彩色木棍，可以是塑料片等，总之每个人的筹码不能相同。这些器物，摆在四方藏桌或卡垫上面，公共筹码在上面堆放成半月形。玩骰子的人，围着藏桌或卡垫席地而坐，可以每个人为一方，也可以两个人为一组。

投骰子的游戏大概分成几个步骤。首先，每个参与游戏的人，轮流把骰子放进木碗，口中念念有词，手不停地摇晃，然后大喝一声，将木碗倒扣在皮垫上面。一般上午年长的人先开头，下午年幼的人开头，同辈的人按顺时针方向开头。第一个人扣下木碗后，第二个人伸手揭开，读出骰子的点数，按点数从后往前拨下相同数目的公共筹码，在那里放两个代表自己的子儿，藏语叫"拉吉"，意思是本金。接着，等打完一轮以后，所有人投完骰子，只能在自己的本金上面，添一个子儿了。这里还有一些规矩和变数。如果打出和上一轮相同的点数，便可以加上一个子儿，还可以再打一次骰子；如果打出的点数，刚好和另一个人的相同，那里已摆放着他的子儿，而他的子儿与自己的相同，或者少于自己的，便可以把他的子儿全部吃掉；如果他的子儿多于自己的子儿，那就输了，只能把自己的子儿撤下来了；另外，凡是投出称为"巴拉"的两点，都被认为是好事，可以重投一次。最后，投骰子的

constantly with two hands, then gives a loud shout, inverts the wooden bowl on the leather cushion. Usually, the senior play first in the morning, the junior play first in the afternoon, and peers play in an order of clockwise. After the first person inverts the wooden bowl, the second person uncovers it, reads the point of the dice, allocates the same number of public chips backwards, and puts two chips there as his principals, which are called "Lajis". After a round is completed, all persons cast the dice, they have to add a chip on their principals. There are some rules and varieties. If the point is the same as the former round, one chip can be added, and one dice can be cast; if the point is the same as that of another person, his chips are placed there and are the same as or less than his, he can eat up all chips of the other person; if those of the other person is more than his, he loses and withdraws his chips; if two points called as "Bala" is cast, it is regarded as a good thing, he can cast again. At last, if one person's nine chips exceed all public chips, he is the winner, and he wades across the river, climbs the mountain and reaches the end point of victory. Victory or defeat of casting dice is victory or defeat of spirit, and has no nature of gambling.

During casting dice, the most interesting thing is gods of casting dice. This represents heavy religious color in Tibetan culture profoundly. There are gods all over Tibet, and everything is blessed by gods. Gods of casting dice are small spirits who are invisible to the naked eyes and are called "Tebulangs", they have five small arrows like Cupid in western myth, shoot people from hidden places and make people breed love, hatred, victory, failure and envy, and these spirits grasp success, failure, victory and defeat of persons casting dice and make wishes and pray for them every now and then. It's said that "Tebulangs" were ancient gods, and they were gods of the Tibetan primitive religion Bonism and gods of witches of Bonism for divination. In this way, the game of casting dice has been inherited in the snow-covered plateau for a long time.

胜负主要看哪个人的九个筹码最先越过所有的公共筹码，趟过河，翻过山，到达胜利的终点，投骰子的胜和负，只是一种精神上的胜负，原本没有什么赌博性质。

在投骰子的过程当中，最有趣的是还有骰子神。这深刻体现了西藏文化当中浓重的宗教色彩。在西藏几乎什么地方都有神，什么事情都有神灵保佑。投骰子的骰子神，是一些很小很小、小到肉眼几乎看不见的小精灵，叫"特布朗"，有点像西方神话中的丘比特，他们有五支小小的箭，从隐秘的地方射到人们的身上，使人们滋生爱情、仇恨、胜利、失败和忌妒，正是这些精灵，掌控着投骰子的输赢胜负。所有投骰子的人，都要时不时地向他们许愿祈祷。据说"特布朗"是非常古老的神，西藏原始宗教苯教的神，也是苯教巫师占卜的神，这样看来，投骰子的游戏应该在雪域高原已经传承非常久远了。

在投骰子的时候，最有意思的还有投骰子的人口中念诵的骰子词。骰子词，藏语叫"晓谐"。投骰子的人不管是比较闹腾的还是比较内向文静的，但念诵骰子词都是少不了的程序。念诵骰子词的目的首先是祈求打出自己需要的点数，其次显示本人渊博的知识和良好的口才，还有活跃气氛的意思。骰子从最小的两点到最大的十二点，每个点数都有固定的或引申的叫法，都有约定俗成的或即兴创作的骰子词。骰子词大多生动有趣，内容丰富，这里援引几首为例。

两点，藏语是"尼巴"，骰子词称为"巴拉"。如：

巴拉来，巴拉来，

巴拉带得吉祥来。

巴拉是吉祥如意的点，

本人是成就胜利的人。

三点，藏语为"松"，引申为"索果"、"索古"（蒙古）等。如：

When casting dice, the most interesting thing also includes dice words chanted by persons casting dice, which are called "Xiaoxie" in Tibetan. No matter persons casting dice are extroverted or introverted, the chanting of dice words is an indispensable procedure, and it aims at praying to cast a point one needs, displaying one's comprehensive knowledge and excellent eloquence, and enlivening entertainment atmosphere. The result of casting ranges from the minimum two points to the maximum twelve points, each point has a fixed or derived name, and has conventional or spontaneous dice words. Most dice words are vivid and interesting, and have rich contents. I take several pieces as examples here.

Point two is called "Niba" in Tibetan, and is called "Bala" in dice words. For example:

Bala comes, Bala comes,

Bala brings good luck.

Bala is the lucky and happy point,

I am the person making success.

Point three is called "Song" in Tibetan, and is derived as "Suoguo" or "Suogu" (Mongolian) etc. For example:

Mongolian Gexi falls from horse back,

He gets the best of the deal from stirrups.

Mongolians eat horsemeat, and even they don't want to eat.

Point five is "A" in Tibetan, and is derived as "Ka" in dice words, means mouth and orientation, and is the harmonic tone of Kangba people and health. For example:

Songs of girls,

Are heard from eastern windows.

Kangba people eat and sleep well,

They have never thought that ghee is stolen by a dog.

Health is bless of living Buhhdas,

Illness is their fate.

Point nine is "Gu" in Tibetan, and is derived as "Kong" (duke) etc. For example:

Witches jump violently,

Fall under God's Table.

Jiangluojin is the highest one among dukes,

Hekang Zhasha is below it.

There is a fire in temple,

Temple attendant's beard is burnt.

Point twelve is called "Jiuni" in Tibetan, and is derived as "Qiang" (north) etc. For example:

Shepherd girls in North Tibet have clever hands,

Milk is sweet with honey.

Rich and colorful contents and humorous and

蒙古格西摔下马背，

省得下镫占了个便宜。

蒙古人吃的是马肉，不想吃马肉也得吃。

五点，藏语为"阿"，骰子词里引申为"卡"，意思是口、朝向，还有康巴人、健康等谐音。如：

朝东的窗户里面，

传出姑娘的歌声。

康巴人吃饱睡得香，

想不到酥油被狗偷。

健康是活佛的保佑，

生病是自己的命运。

九点，藏语为"古"，引申成"空"（公）等。例如：

女巫蹦跳过猛，

栽到神桌底下。

公爵里最高的是江洛金，

这下面是霍康札萨。

神殿里面失了火，

庙祝的胡子被烧焦。

十二点，藏语叫"久尼"，引申为"羌"（北方）等。如：

藏北的牧女双手巧，

挤出的牛奶带蜜糖。

骰子词丰富多彩的内

容和幽默风趣的风格给投骰子的游戏增添了不少乐趣，更是一笔难得的民族文化的财富。

funny styles add a lot of fun to the game of casting dice, and are hard-won wealth of ethnic culture.

第四章
藏区各地藏历年的习俗

　　从文化概念上来看，藏地实际上是一个很宽泛的概念。从大的范围来划分，藏区至少可以分成三个文化区：第一个以西藏自治区为主除掉昌都地区的卫藏，卫藏又可分成阿里、前藏、后藏三个区域，拉萨则是前藏的核心，而后藏是以日喀则为中心；第二个区域称为康区，范围大概是西藏自治区的昌都地区、那曲东部、林芝地区东部，青海省的玉树藏族自治州，四川省的甘孜藏族自治州和云南省的迪庆藏族自治州，这些地方的藏族大多是操康方言，所以通常把这些地方称为"康藏"；第三个区域是安多藏区，大致包括青海的海北、海南、黄南、果洛四个藏族自治州，甘肃西南部的甘南藏族自治州以及四川藏族羌族自治州北部的藏族区域，这些地方的藏族操安多方言，所以叫安多藏区。虽然这些区域从最大的范围来说都是藏区，但实际上他们的语言、宗教包括风土人情都是存在一定区别的。所以藏地的文化有着很强烈的多样性。就从过藏历年来说，在藏地各个不同的区域欢庆藏历新年的活动大致相似，到这个章节就要介绍不同地区的藏族过藏历年有哪些不同的地方，来充分反映各地文化的特色和藏地文化的多样性。

Chapter Four

Conventions of Tibetan New Year in the Tibetan Areas

In terms of culture, the concept of the Tibetan areas is very broad. On a large scale, the Tibetan areas can be divided into three cultural zones: the first zone is Central Tibet, which can be subdivided into Ali, Anterior Tibet and Posterior Tibet, Lhasa is the core of Anterior Tibet and Posterior Tibet uses Shigatse as the center; the second zone is called Kang Region, roughly covers Qamdo Prefecture, east Nagqu and east Nyingchi Prefecture, Yushu Tibetan Autonomous Prefecture in Qinghai Province, Garze Tibetan Autonomous Prefecture in Sichuan Province and Deqen Tibetan Autonomous Prefecture in Yunnan Province, and most Tibetans in these areas speak in Kang dialect, so these places are called Kang Tibet; the third zone is Amdo Tibetan Region, includes Haibei, Hainan, Huangnan and Guoluo Tibetan Autonomous Prefectures in Qinghai, Gannan Tibetan Autonomous Prefecture in southwest Gansu and the Tibetan region in north Sichuan Tibetan and Qiang Autonomous Prefecture, Tibetans in these places speak Amdo dialect, so it is called Amdo Tibetan Region. Although these regions are the Tibetan areas in the largest scope, there are certain differences among their languages, religions, customs and practices. Therefore, Tibetan culture has strong diversifications. In terms of celebrating Tibetan New Year, celebration activities held in different Tibetan areas are roughly similar. In this chapter, I will introduce differences among Tibetans in different areas to celebrate Tibetan New Year, which can reflect characteristics of cultures in different places and varieties of Tibetan culture.

1

日喀则的藏历年
Tibetan New Year in Shigatse

Shigatse is the core area of Posterior Tibet, it has a vast territory and an intriguing culture, people are simple and honest, and Tibetan New Year is celebrated here in a way which is similar to Lhasa, but there are certain differences. In Shigatse, traditional New Year was earlier than Lhasa in the past, which was called "Suolang Losar", meaning "Peasant New Year", and it began on the first day of the twelfth month in the Tibetan calendar and was one month ahead of Tibetan New Year in Lhasa. However, most places in Shigatse celebrate Tibetan New Year in the first month nowadays.

Preparation before Celebrating New Year

Usually, Shigatse begins to prepare for Tibetan New Year since the early December. On the twenty-

日喀则是后藏的核心地区，这里地域辽阔，文化底蕴厚重，民风淳朴，这里过藏历年的与拉萨地区大致相同，但是也有一定的差异。在日喀则，过去传统的新年比拉萨早，称为"索朗洛萨"，意为"农民新年"，时间是藏历的十二月一日开始，比拉萨的藏历年提前了一个月。不过，现在日喀则的大部分地区藏历新年基本上都统一到了正月来过。

过年前的准备

日喀则过藏历年现在一般也是从十二月初开始

准备。在十二月二十九这天，要举行"古恰"的活动，即把室内室外彻底打扫干净。在院子里燃起一大堆火，让烟雾弥漫整个山谷。此外，要在屋的正厅、窗户、厨房等的梁、门、壁、柱和木斗拱上，用土碱或糌粑画上表示吉祥的八吉祥图。男人将家里东西北三个方向所象征密宗事部三怙主的佛部文殊、金刚部金刚手和莲花部观音的"玛尼堆"用白漆、红土、烟汁涂成白、红、黑三色，然后，男人要洗"古扎思令江巴"头。人们认为男人们在这天洗头，家里会吉祥，工作会如意，头发会长得又黑又长。但是，与拉萨那边不太相同的是，妇女在这一天是不许洗头的，因为在日喀则，人们认为妇女在这一天洗头是不吉利的。同时，媳妇和女儿不管是谁，都要把新年初一早晨做粥的小麦砸成扁状，阿妈用面团粘净衣饰以及家畜的套颈索和耳饰上的灰土，洗净坐垫、小茶几、藏柜、大小银碗、

ninth day of the twelfth month, the activity of "Guqia" is held, which means cleaning indoors and outdoors thoroughly. A big fire is burnt in the yard, and the whole valley is filled with smoke. Moreover, eight auspicious things which represent luck are drawn on beams, doors, columns, and wooden bucket arches on atriums, windows and kitchens of houses with alkaline earth or Zanba. Men paint "Nimadui" of Manjusri in Buddha family, Vajra-dhara in Vajra family and Avalokitesvara in Padma family who symbolize three great masters in Kriya Tantra of Esoteric Buddhism in the east, west and north of the house into white, red and black with white paint, red clay and soot, then they wash their hair called "Guzha Siling Jiangba". It is thought that if men wash hair on this day, family will become auspicious, works will become lucky, and hair will become black and long. However, women aren't allowed to wash hair on this day, which differs from Lhasa, because it is thought that women's washing hair on this day is unpropitious in Shigatse. Meanwhile, either daughters-in-law or daughters smash wheat which is used for porridge into flat shape, mothers clean dust on clothes, ornaments, neck cords of livestock, and earrings with flour, clean cushions, small end tables, Tibetan cabinets, big and small silver bowls, wild ox horns, Zanba moulds etc., and prepare offering being sacrificed to gods, fried foods, "Qiema", wine, tea and ginseng fruit.

野牛角、糌粑模子等，还
要把敬神用的供品、油炸
食品、"切玛"、酒新、
茶、人参果预备好。

二十九日晚驱邪

Expelling Evils on the Twenty-ninth Day

On the twenty-ninth day, the ceremony of driving ghosts is held in Shigatse, and the procedures are similar to those in Lhasa, but the specific processes are different somewhat. On the evening of the twenty-ninth day, a substitute is put in a pottery pot without two ears, i.e. a "female" ghost which is made of tea leaves, lees, peppers, turnips, dust and soil and so on. After preparation, offerings are placed in front of Buddha images in the house, mother and father begin to fill a bowl with gnocchi soup for everyone, all people drink three sips, then pour the rest to the pottery pot storing the ghost substitute. They say when pouring, "I have eaten new porridge, then give the rest to you, one, two and three," then pour the porridge into the pot little by little for nine times and begin to expel evils.

Expelling evils means that one pitches a little of dough in his or her hand, seals fingerprint on it clearly, and makes it into a slim round, and prays that, "Take away the evil, take away the evil, there are twelve months and three hundred and sixty

在二十九日这一天，
日喀则也要进行驱鬼仪
式，环节大致与拉萨的相
似，但在具体过程中有些
不同。二十九日晚上，要
在一个断了两耳柄的陶罐
里放一个替身物品——用
熬过的茶叶、酒糟、辣
椒、萝卜、烟土等捏成的
"女鬼"。准备好以后，
先在家里的佛像前摆上供
品，再由阿爸阿妈开头，
往各人碗里盛上满满一碗
面块汤，大家都喝三口，
然后把剩余的往放鬼替身
的陶罐里倒，边倒边说：
"新粥我吃了，剩下的给
你，一、二、三。"再将
新粥向罐里一点一点地倒
九次后开始驱邪。

驱邪是拿一点揉好
的面捏在手心里，把手印
清楚地印上去，捏成一个
瘦形的圆形状，嘴里祈
祷说："带走邪气，带

走邪气，一年十二个月三百六十天，魔鬼、波折、病痛、战争、灾荒、霜冻、冰雹等灾害一个不留地全部消除。"接着诅咒："洗的话没有不洁白的，熏的话没有不干净的，我背的话比一根羊毛还轻，你背的话比一根金子还重。"说完各自把衣服的下摆撕下一丝线，把"替身"包起来，吐一口口水，用锅底或灶里的烟灰抹成黑色，放进罐子里；有的村寨还给家畜驱邪。

驱邪完后，接着把"替身"送到屋外去，大概就是晚上九点的时候，开始用火把赶鬼。一个男人拿一把禾结，用火点燃。从正屋开始，不分里屋外屋地用火熏，一边熏，一边说："出来吧，出来吧。"一直赶到门外。同时一个女人在火把的前面拿着"替身"，摔在三岔路口。男人像驱邪魔一样放火药枪，如果拿替身的女人身上燃着了一点火，就象征着这地方的女鬼、饿鬼、妖魔、独脚

days in a year, and all disasters such as monster, setback, disease, war, famine, frost, hail etc. shall be eliminated." Then one curses that, "It becomes pure and white if it is washed, it becomes clean if it is fumigated, it is lighter than a piece of fleece if I carry it, and it is heavier than a piece of gold if you carry it." After saying, everyone takes a piece of thread from his or her clothes, wraps the "substitute", spits at it, smears it into black with soot taken from bottom of pan or stove, and puts it into the pot; and some villages even expel evils for livestock.

After expelling evils, people send "the substitute" outside houses, and begin to drive ghosts with torches at nine o'clock in the evening. A man fires a handful of faggots, starts from main building to fumigate houses one by one, he says when fumigating, "Come out, come out," and drives them outdoors. Meanwhile, a woman picks up "the substitute" in front of the torch, and throws it to three-way intersection. Man fires a power shotgun like driving evils and monsters. If there is a fire on the woman carrying the torch, it symbolizes that disease, pain, war, famine etc. caused by female ghosts, hungry ghosts, evil spirits, one-foot ghosts and outdoors monsters are eliminated. Arriving at place sending ghosts with torches, young men fire juniper branches and plant stems with the sound of firecrackers, the torches illuminate the whole ditch, and they shout at the female ghost, "The old woman with a broken gourd ladle, Boo Hoo! The old woman with black breast and heavy head, Boo Hoo! The old woman with black buttocks eating peas, Boo Hoo! The old woman eating raw paste, Boo Hoo!"

When driving ghosts with torch, the old mother and daughters-in-law meet them at back of the door. The man with the torch brings back a white stone called "sacred stone" to the old mother, she asks the man with the sacred stone before he enters the house, "Where are you from?" The man answers, "I come from my favorite place." She asks again, "I carry the luck treasure with me, then where are you going to?" The man answers, "I am going to the happy place." After answering, the man gives the "sacred stone" to the mother, and she sticks ghee flowers on the "sacred stone", and the daughter-in-law offers "new wine" to him. Meanwhile, the father makes a start, and everyone pours barley wine into large wooden bowls, moves in circles and drinks it pleasantly. After drinking, "Qiema" is offered. Auspicious ghee flowers are stuck on their right shoulders, and Hadas are hung on the neck of the man who brought back the "sacred stone"

鬼以及室外鬼妖作怪造成的病痛、战争、灾荒等一个不留全部消除掉了。到了用火把送鬼的地方,青年们一边点燃刺柏树枝和植物杆,伴随着火爆声,火光把整个山沟照得一片通明,一边对女鬼起哄:"腰间别着缺口瓢的老太婆,呜呜!黑奶头重的老太婆,呜呜!吃豌豆的黑屁股老太婆,呜呜!食生面糊的老太婆,呜呜!"

用火把送鬼的人们回来时,老妈妈和媳妇在房门后迎接他们。拿火把的男子带回一个叫"神石"的白石头交给老阿妈,阿妈没等带神石的男子进屋就问:"你从哪里来?"男子道:"我从喜欢的地方来。"阿妈又问:"我带着如意宝,现在你到哪儿去?"男子答道:"我到幸福地方去。"问答完毕,把"神石"交到阿妈手里,阿妈在"神石"上黏上酥油花,媳妇给他献上"新酒"。同时从老阿爸开始,用大木碗斟上青稞酒,转着圈尽情地喝。喝完酒,都献上"切玛"。在大家的右肩黏上吉祥的酥油花，在带回"神石"的男子的脖子上挂着表示英雄的哈达。老阿妈把"神石"供献在正室生日神或者护法神的跟前，当作家里的宝贝。

吃"古吐"

火把送鬼完后，大家按座次坐好，也开始喝面疙瘩汤——"古吐"。吃"古吐"依然是一家人最开心的时刻。所有人都不希望自己碗里有背小孩的面疙瘩，因为这表示那人在外面有搞出私生子的危险；也不希望吃到有鼓的面疙瘩，说那个人会在朋友之间挑拨离间；更不希望吃到有木炭的面疙瘩，这表示那人有一颗黑心；吃到有背青稞的面疙瘩，表示这人容易得传染病；吃到歪脖子懒汉，表示那人对工作又怕又懒……而所有人都希望自己吃到月亮的面疙瘩，表示那人的心像天空中的月亮一样明亮；吃到太阳的面疙瘩，表示那人的福气

symbolizing hero. The old mother offers the "sacred stone" in front of Birthday God or Dharmapala in the main room, and the stone is regarded as a treasure at home.

Eating "Gutu"

After driving ghosts with torches, all the people are seated according to the order of seats and begin to eat Gutu, which is dough ball soup. Eating "Gutu" is still the happiest time for a family. One doesn't hope to have dough balls having images of children in his or her bowls, because it symbolizes that he or she has the danger to have an illegitimate child; one doesn't hope to have dough balls with drum, which represents that he or she drives a wedge among friends; one doesn't want to eat dough balls with charcoal, which represents he or she has a black heart; if one eats dough balls having images of barley, he or she is easy to get an infection; if one eats dough balls which are shaped as idlers with wry necks, he or she is afraid of works and is lazy. However, one hopes to eat moon-like dough balls, which symbolizes that his or her heart is as bright as the moon in the sky; one hopes to eat sun-like dough balls, which symbolizes that he or she has good luck; if one eats dough balls shaped like three jewels of supreme master, which symbolizes that he or she is pure and good-hearted; if one eats dough balls shaped like small quadrangular pads, which symbolizes that he or she will become religious believers. All members eat while talking in this way, and the whole family is always filled with happy laughter.

On the last day of the year, which is called "the last day full of burnt odor", men go to ridges or steep rocks which are far from home to burn sheep heads which will be sacrificed on the morning of the first day of the first month.

Taboos and Activities on the First Day

On the morning of the first day of the first month, there is just a suspicion of light in the east, daughter-in-law or the elderly daughter gets up to stew wine rather than porridge, which differs from that in Lhasa. When the cock crows for the first time, the stewed wine is sent to the places where family members sleep. After drinking one or two bowls of wine, you will be fined to drink three more bowls if you say, "I don't want to drink now"; if you say that you are full and cannot drink any more, the wine will be poured on your head, then everyone continues to sleep.

When the cock has crowed for three times, some families bring "Qiema" and Zanba to take the "four new things", i.e. "new ox dung" from cow dung from other houses, "new land" from land which has been plowed in summer, "new water" from

大; 吃到有上师三宝的面疙瘩, 表示那人心地洁白善良; 吃到有四方形小垫的面疙瘩, 表示那人可成为宗教徒。一家人边吃边这样说着, 整个家里总是充满欢声笑语。

而岁末的最后一天, 也叫做"弥漫焦臭的最后一天"。男子要到离家很远的土坎陡岩边去烧焦大年初一早上敬献的羊头。

初一的禁忌与活动

大年初一的早上, 东方刚发白, 和拉萨不一样的是家里的媳妇或大女儿要起床熬酒而不是麦片粥。鸡叫头遍的时候, 把熬好的酒送到家人睡的地方。喝了一两碗酒后, 你若说"现在不喝了", 就会被罚三碗; 如果你说喝饱了, 再也喝不下去的话, 就会把酒倒在你的头上, 然后大家接着睡觉。

鸡叫三遍的时候, 有些人家带着"切玛"、糌粑去取"四新"——从别人家牛粪里取"牛粪新", 从夏种地里取"土新"，从水源处取"水新"，从狗窝里取"粪新"。在取"四新"时，要在上述四个地方撒些糌粑粉。对其他来抓取"四新"的人，作为惩罚要浇他一瓢水，因此得有一个人要给取"四新"的人放哨。如果看到其他人家来抓"四新"，立刻发出暗号，叫他快逃。取"四新"的人回到自己家里，给"土新"粘上酥油花，供奉在男神跟前；把"水新"放在正屋的护法神跟前，当作供水供上；将"牛粪新"粘上酥油花，放进牛棚，"粪新"粘上酥油花，放在厕所里。这种活动表示能防止霜灾雹害和招财引福。

天快亮时，男女青年一个个打扮得相当漂亮，一些人到山岗上插风马旗，一些人去取"手纹水新"，即天还未亮，但手纹能看清楚时去取"水新"。到山上去插风旗的人们带着在柳枝上缀着彩绫、彩色羊毛线、彩色羊毛的风旗和神香"切玛"、糌粑面、青

water source, and "new dung" from doghouse. When taking the "four new things", one throws Zanba powder to these four places. As for another person who comes to grasp "four new things", he will be poured a gourd of water as punishment, so one person needs to guard the one taking the "four new things". If he sees other family coming to take the "four new things", the guarder will send the high signal to withdraw. When the persons who take the "four new things" come back, "new land" will be stuck with ghee flowers and be sacrificed in front of male gods; "new water" will be put in front of Dharmapala in the main house, and will be sacrificed as the offered water; "new ox dung" will be stuck with ghee flowers and put into the cowshed; "new dung" will be stuck with ghee flowers and put into the toilet. This kind of activity can prevent frost and hail disasters and bring wealth and luck.

Men and women dress up before daybreak, some people come to hillocks to erect wind-horse flags, some people come to take "fingerprints and new water", that is to say, one comes to take "new water" just when fingerprints can be seen clearly before daybreak. People who climb hills to erect wind-horse flags carry them with colored silk threads, wool yarns, the sacred incense "Qiema", Zanba flour, and barley wine, and they burn incense at the top of hillocks, erect wind-horse flags and pray for better luck. However, persons taking "fingerprints and new water" are old mothers, daughters-in-law and children usually. After dressing up, they tie Hada or white and clean wool on the neck of water bucket or leather bucket with ghee flowers stuck on the bucket mouth, and carry sacred incense, Qiema, Zanba powder, colored wools and barley wine etc. After arriving at the place of taking "new water", they hang colored wools on trees on the banks of the river, which are like colorful rainbow, and burn incense to sacrifice to water gods, then children begin to play games. Some of them dance, some of them sing, some of them dance for gods, some of them kick shuttlecock and so on.

When the sun rises, "new water" which is called "Nixia Qubei" needs to be taken. When new water of "Nixia Qubei" is taken, besides elderly family members, children also dress up well. They make a circle knot on water bucket with Hada or wool, stick ghee flowers on bucket mouth, and come to take "new water" with sacred incense, Qiema and Zanba powder. Before taking "new water", they come to the banks of the river to burn incense and sacrifice to "new water". It's said that it's a lucky sign to make the time to fill the last guard of water consistent with the time when the sun rises from the top of the mountain, and it's an unlucky sign to make the time when filling the water bucket not consistent with the

稞酒，在山岗高高的顶上烧香，插风旗，祈求运气越来越好。而去取"手纹水新"的一般是家里的老阿妈、媳妇和小孩。他们打扮一新后，在水桶或皮桶的脖子上系上哈达或白净的羊毛，在桶口上粘酥油花，带上神香、切玛、糌粑粉、彩色羊毛、青稞酒等，到达取"水新"的地方后，把彩色羊毛挂在河两岸的树上，就像彩虹一样七彩纷呈，然后烧香祭礼水神，祭礼水神后，小孩子开始玩游戏，有的跳舞，有的唱歌，有的跳神，有的踢毽子，等等。

早晨太阳升起时，还要取叫做"尼夏曲被"的"水新"，取"尼夏曲被"水新时，家里除了阿爸阿妈外，其他孩子也要穿戴好，在水桶上用哈达或羊毛打成一个圆圈结，在桶口粘上酥油花，带上神香、切玛和糌粑粉，然后去取"水新"。取"水新"前，先在河岸边烧香祭祀"水新"，装水时，太阳在山顶露出笑脸的时间要和装满水桶最后一瓢水的时间一致，据说这是办事有运气的征兆，如果太阳在山顶升起的时间和装满水桶的时间不一致的话，就会不吉利，取"尼夏曲被"水新的时候，是和邻居、乡亲们一块去的，装满水后，姑娘们各自玩耍去。

上述活动告一段落，家人要聚在一起，首先是父母，然后是兄弟姐妹，按长幼秩序给每个人献上新年鲜花和用彩色酥油装饰的"竹素切玛"，献的人说："吉祥如意。"受献的人说："吉祥如意，圆满昌盛，阿妈贵体安康，长长久久获得安乐，明年这个时候，生机勃勃再相见。"

在日喀则地区，初一这一天有很多禁忌的习俗。譬如，新年第一天的早晨，不能把牛粪扔到外面，不能把外边的客人叫到家里，不能到别人家里做客，也不能把家里的东西借出去。假如把牛粪扔到外边，把东西借给别人，会失去马、牛、羊的财运，会失去五谷的营

time when the sun rises from the mountain. When taking the new water of "Nixia Qubei", neighbors and villagers come together, and girls play on their own after the water is acquired.

When the above activity is completed, family members get together. Firstly, parents offer "Zhusu Qiema" which is decorated with New Year flowers and colored ghee, and then siblings offer it according to the order from the senior to the junior. The offering person says, "Good luck", the person being offered says, "Good luck, prosperity, wish mother be healthy and happy for ever, and meet with each other vigorously."

In Shigatse Region, there are many taboo conventions on the first day. For example, ox dung cannot be thrown outside on the morning of the first day of New Year, outside guests cannot be invited to home, one cannot be a guest at other's home, and things cannot be lent. If ox dung is thrown outside, things are lent to others, people will lose fortune of horse, ox and sheep and nutrition of five cereals and cannot become rich. On the morning of the first day, parents cannot scold children or swear, and they shall fill the water vast carefully so that water cannot spill out, otherwise it is an unlucky symbol.

On the morning of the first day, which is called "the first day of sleekness", oil is smeared on heads of children, soot and oil are mixed and smeared on horns of livestocks, and lees are fed to them. Rich families use Tibetan lees to feed them, then they also become drunk. "New wine" and "Zhusu Qiema" are offered to livestock as well, ghee flowers are struck on horns, their earrings and neck cords are exchanged newly. The mother traverses the sheet called "five-treasure cape" on the right shoulder and prays, "The local land gods perceive, the home gods perceive, there are no war, famine, frost or hail, heaven rain falls in good time, rainfall is favorable, there are wealth, happiness and prosperity, people and animals are healthy and sound." Correspondingly, people sacrifice to heavenly gods, "Zan" gods on earth and dragon gods underground.

After the above activities, people begin to have breakfast. Parents give everyone in the family a portion of meat: a plate of meat, a sheep head and

养，永远也富不了。初一的早晨，阿爸阿妈也不能骂孩子、说粗话，甚至要非常注意地把水缸装得满满的，但不能溢到外面去，否则也是不吉利的象征。

初一早晨，也叫"初一油光光"，不但要给孩子头上抹许多油，还把烟灰和油混合起来，把家畜的角抹得亮光光的，挤出酒糟给家畜，富裕人家还用藏酒醪糟喂家畜，让家畜也大醉，给家畜献"酒新"和"竹素切玛"，在角尖上粘上酥油花，还把家畜的耳饰和旧颈套换成新的，这时阿妈把右肩上的叫做"五宝帔"的披单横着祈祷说："本地的地神明鉴，家中的家神明鉴，没有战争和饥荒，没有霜冻和雹灾，天雨适时降下，年景雨水常常调匀，财富福禄昌盛，人畜安康无恙。"相应还祭祀天上的天神、地上的"赞"神、地下的龙神。

上面活动完后，就开始吃早饭。阿爸阿妈给家中所有的人一份肉：一盘肉，一个羊头，一块血肠。分完肉，阿妈把五升粮酿的青稞酒放在座次的中间，在酒壶和壶口边粘上三大朵酥油花，上面横放一把酒瓢，媳妇或大女儿拿着酒壶，从父母开始，轮流着一杯又一杯地敬。喝完酒之后，和拉萨地区同样地全家人围在一起吃麦片粥。只是喝完麦片粥，又要开始喝饭后酒。饭后酒是放在大木碗和牛角里，斟的酒要喝得一滴不剩，如果木碗里剩下一滴酒，就要罚"滴酒"，再倒一大碗。饭余酒后，人们喜欢玩什么，就玩什么。过段时间，开始吃小午饭，他们给老人在小木碗和瓷盘里摆上油炸点心、烤饼、荞面饼、麻花等，让他们吃好。中午十二点时，吃"怕察玛库"或肉馍馍。晚上吃面疙瘩汤。

初二、初三日

在初二这天吃完早饭后，家里老人带着孩子去祭祀土地神和护法神。

a piece of blood sausage. After distributing meat, mother places barley wine in the middle of seats which is brewed from five liters of grain, and three big ghee flowers are struck on the wine pot and pot mouth, a wine gourd is placed on it, daughter-in-law or elderly daughter picks up the wine pot, and toast one by one from parents. After drinking wine, the whole family members sit around to eat cereal in the same way as that in Lhasa. After having cereal, they begin to drink after-meal wine, which is filled in a wooden bowl and an ox horn, and they shall drink up the wine. If there is a drop of wine left in the wooden bowl, one will be fined because of "drop of wine", and another big bowl will be filled up. After having meal and drinking wine, people play as they like. After a while, they begin to have lunch, they place fried pastries, hot cakes, buckwheat cakes, and hemp flowers etc. in small wooden bowls and porcelain plates for old men, and let them help themselves. At noon, they eat "Pacha Maku" or meat bun. They eat dough ball soup in the evening.

The Second and Third Days

After the breakfast on the second day, old people lead children to sacrifice to land gods and Dharmapalas. Since local people and neighbors will get together in places of sacrificing to land gods and Dharmapalas, each family dress up with the best clothes and ornaments, and bring barley wine and various kinds of fried foods. When they arrive at the place of sacrificing to land gods, one old man collects sacred incenses, "Qiema" and Zanba powder, offers "new wine" and makes a big sacred incense stack. A young man climbs on the place where flags will be erected for land gods to erect them, lines up, sacrifices to land gods and prays in a high voice, "Jiji Suosuo, wish good gods victory! A good harvest!" After sacrificing to land gods, they sacrifice to Dharmapalas. When sacrificing Dharmapalas, they shall bring sacred lamps and Hadas. When worshiping Buddhas, one boy takes "Zhusu Qiema" in his hand, one girl holds wine pot, and they pay New Year calls to villagers, neighbors, relatives and friends nearby.

On the third day, people sacrifice to gods by offering sacred incenses on the roofs of their houses and erect prayer flags for good luck according to their economic conditions. Since the third day, guests can be invited to their houses, they can be guests of others. Relatives, friends and lovers shall be invited to their houses, and three meals are treated grandly each day.

由于当地人和左邻右舍都要聚集在祭祀土地神和护法神的地方，每一家人都用最好的服饰打扮起来，带上青稞酒和各类油炸食品。到了祭祀土地神的地方，一个老年人把神香和"切玛"糌粑粉集中在一起，献上"酒新"，然后做好一个大的神香堆。一个小伙子爬上土地神插旗的地方，插上风旗，排好队，声音高亢地祭祀土地神并祈祷说："吉吉唆唆，愿善神得胜喽！好丰年喽！"祭祀土地神完后，去祭护法神。祭护法神时，要带上神灯、哈达。朝佛的同时，一个男孩手里拿着"竹素切玛"，一个女孩子手里捧着酒壶，向在附近的乡亲、邻居、亲戚、朋友拜年。

到了初三，根据家里经济情况，在自家屋顶献上神烟祭神，插上招来运气的经幡。从初三起，可以请客人到家里，家里人也可以到别人家做客，尤其是亲戚、朋友、恋人都要请到家里，每天隆重地招待三餐。

新年要过几天，根据地方风俗和条件来定，没有固定的期限。过完年的那天晚上，有些人家要举办"新年散宴"，尽可能地把家里人、邻居、亲戚、男女朋友以及能歌善舞的男女聚集起来，摆上"切玛"、糌粑粉、五升粮食的酒，唱歌，跳舞。酒宴完后，每人拈上一点"竹素切玛"里面的糌粑粉，声音高亢地祈祷说："吉吉唆唆，愿善神得胜！"

日喀则人的新年盛装

日喀则人过年的时候的打扮也很有讲究。一般中年妇女在过年的日子里，外面通常穿一件无袖长袍，罩着里面的皮袍，领口、袖头则翻出里面天蓝、紫色等素色衬衫。腰上围一条彩虹般的"帮典"，脚上蹬一双自家做的高腰氆氇镶呢藏靴（松巴拉姆）。老年妇女不戴首饰，却要穿上大红的衬衣。不论中年还是老年妇

New Year is held for several days, which is decided by local conventions and conditions, and there is no fixed term. On the evening of New Year celebration, some families hold "New Year departing feast", try to get family members, neighbors, relatives, friends, men and women who are good at singing and dancing together, place "Qiema", Zanba powder, and wine made from five liters of grain, sing songs and dance. After the feast, everyone picks up a little of Zanba powder in "Zhusu Qiema" and prays in a high voice, "Jiji Suosuo, wish good gods victory!"

Splendid New Year Dresses of Shigatse People

Shigatse people pay particular attention to dresses. Usually, middle-aged women wear gowns without sleeves, which cover furred robe and collar, and cuffs expose their shirts, which often have plain blue, purple or other light colors. They wear a rainbow "Bangdian" on waist, and a pair of high Tibetan boots with wool made by themselves (Songba Lamu). Old women don't wear ornaments, but wear bright red shirts. Either middle-aged women or old women wear two braids of "Zhaxiu". Unmarried young girls don't wear "Bangdian", but wear single braid, and their colors of "Zhaxiu" are brighter, and their shirts are more colorful. Urban girls like to wear "Songba Lamu", and some of them wear a pair of better and brighter shoes.

Men like to wear "Ciren Jinguo" (Tibetan embroidered satin caps with big edges in the front and at the back) or leather caps, large gowns, and colors of gowns are darkened with ages. In the past, men wore braids, black golden suede boot to match with clothes and ornaments all over.

女，一概都梳着两根系着"扎秀"的辫子。年轻的未婚姑娘不围"帮典"，辫着独辫，"扎秀"颜色更鲜，衬衣的花色也五花八门。城里的姑娘不仅爱穿"松巴拉姆"，有的还要穿一双式样较好、擦得发亮的皮鞋。

男人们喜欢头戴"次仁金果"（前后各有一大沿，顶上是绣花缎子的藏式帽子）或皮帽，身穿大袍，只不过随年龄的增加加深袍子的颜色罢了。过去时兴男人扎辫子时，他们曾穿过黑色金丝绒靴，用以搭配全身的服饰。

2 工布藏区的新年
New Year in Gongbo Tibetan Region

工布藏区包括现今行政区划的林芝县、米林县、工布江达县一带。历史上习惯称这里为工布地区，这块区域直到20世纪50年代川藏公路通车之前，仍然森林密布、道路艰险、交通闭塞，山民们以打猎、伐木、采集野果和播种青稞、豌豆、荞麦维持生活。他们的服装、语言、生产方式、风俗习惯都有自己的特点。他们的新年也不是在藏历正月初一过，而是在藏历十月初一过。关于为什么在这个时候过年，工布人有自己的说法。

Gongbo Tibetan Region includes Nyingchi County, Mainling County and Gongbo'gyamda County in the administrative region, which was called Gongbo Region historically. Sichuan-Tibet Road wasn't open to traffic before 1950s, the region was full of forests, roads were dangerous, traffic was blocked, and people hunted, cut wood, collected wild fruits, sowed barley, bean and buckwheat to make their living. Their clothes, languages, production models, and conventions have had their own characteristics. They celebrate New Year on the first day of the tenth month, rather than the first day of the first month. Why do they celebrate New Year on this day? Gongbo people have their own reasons.

It was said that people celebrated New Year on the first day of the first month in the Tibetan calendar here like Lhasa Region. In the era of Gongbo King Ajie Jiebo, there was a strong team of foreign enemies, and they approached north Gongbo frontier. Gongbo King wanted to lead all men to leave their hometown for fighting. "Adas" (a general term for Gongbo men) were unable to part from their hometown, because it was deep fall, and wasn't far from New Year celebration. New Year celebration was very attractive to them, because they can drink old barley wine, eat fat pork and roasted wheat cakes, and sit around the fire of old oriental white oak timbers and dance "Bo", i.e. the local folk dance. Ajie Jiebo was a clever leader, saw through the mind of Adas, and declared loudly, "Oh! Adas! We shall fight as well as celebrate New Year. If we don't fight, we shall not celebrate New Year; if we don't celebrate New Year, we will be no in mood to fight. I make the decision that New Year of Gongbo Region will be celebrated on the first day of the tenth month! You eat and drink fully, enjoy yourselves pleasantly, and then you set out to fight!" Gongbo men celebrated New Year in advance, so they felt happy, fought bravely and won victory. From then on, New Year has been celebrated on the first day of the tenth month in the Tibetan calendar in Gongbo region, and this convention has descended to today.

传说早先这里跟拉萨地区一样，也是藏历正月初一过年。到了工布王阿杰结波时代，有一支强大的外敌，迫近工布北部边境。工布王要带领所有的男人离开家乡去打仗，"阿达"们（对工布男子的泛称）却有点恋恋不舍，当时已是深秋，离过年的时间不远了。过年，要喝老青稞煮的酒，啃老肥猪的肉，吃老麦子烤的饼，还要围着老青杠木燃起的篝火跳当地的民间舞"博"，这些对他们有很强的吸引力。阿杰结波是个聪明的首领，看出了阿达们的心思，便大声地宣布："哟！阿达们！仗不能不打，年也不能不过。不打仗，过不了年；不过年，也没有心思打仗。我决定，工布地区的年，提前到十月初一来过！你们吃得饱饱的，喝得足足的，玩得痛痛快快的，再出发打仗吧！"据说，工布的男人们提前过了年，心里痛快，打仗也卖力气，最后取得了胜利。从此，工布地区就在藏历十月初一过年，这个习俗一直传到今天。

赶鬼

工布藏区的新年赶鬼不是在二十九晚上，而是在三十晚上。到了藏历九月三十日傍晚，家家户户都"赶鬼"，不让鬼扰乱新年活动。工布人赶鬼，很有森林地区的特点。房主人举着火苗呼呼的松明，跑进每一间屋子，从怀里抓出早已准备好的拇指大的白石子和黑石子，哗哗啦啦地朝角落里砸过去，口里不停地喊："折！古哇！"（意为"鬼！等着瞧！"）有的人家，还朝火炬上泼烧酒，火炬上立刻腾起极高的火焰，发出嘶嘶的啸声，赶鬼仪式显得更有气势。当他们认为所有的"鬼"确实已逃出了自己的房子时，赶紧用松枝和旺波树干把门挡严实。工布人认为，这样，"鬼"无法再回来，他们就可以快快乐乐地欢度新年了。

Driving Ghosts

New Year ghost-driving isn't held on the evening of the twenty-ninth day, but is held on the evening of the thirtieth day in Gongbo Tibetan Region. On the evening of September 30 in the Tibetan calendar, every household drives ghosts, and doesn't allow ghosts to disturb New Year activities. Gongbo people's driving ghosts has the characteristics of forest areas. House masters hold flaming pine torches, run into every house, grasp thumb-sized white and black stones from their bosoms which are prepared in advance, cast them towards corners and shout continuously, "Zhe! Guwa!" (meaning "Ghosts! Wait and see!") Some families pour liquor to torches, and very high flame is rised up from the torches at once with a hissing sound, which makes ghost-driving ceremony more powerful. When they think that all "ghosts" have escaped from their houses, they block doors with pine branches and Wangpo trunks tightly. Gongbo people think that "ghosts" will not come back in this way, and they can celebrate New Year happily.

Inviting Dogs for Feast

After driving ghosts, households invite dogs for feast. This is a characteristic content in New Year of Gongbo Region. They place foods which are used to celebrate New Year on wooden trays and plates orderly, which include Zanba dumplings, beef, mutton, pork, peach, walnut, ghee, milk residue, ginseng fruit, barley wine and so on. Tea and wine are filled in walnut shells. After preparation, masters invite dogs and say, "Comfortable and happy dogs, please dine!" Being invited three times, dogs begin to eat. Some dogs bark, overturn plates, tea and wine, masters think that it's unlucky and they drive off this kind of unfavorable "honored guests". Gongbo people think that treating dogs is instructions of gods, so the whole family members are extremely concerned, and stare at each action of dogs. Eating Zanba or cake predicates grain harvest; eating ghee or milk residue predicates prosperity of animal husbandry. They shall not eat meat, if dogs eat meat on the evening of the thirtieth day, people will die or there will be a plague. Strangely, dogs seldom eat meat on the evening of this day, and I don't know what prevention measures Gongbo people have taken.

请狗赴宴

赶完了鬼，家家户户请狗吃饭。这是工布地区新年非常有特色的一项内容。他们把过年的食物，端端正正地放在木盘里，摆在长长的木板上，有糌粑团、牛羊猪肉，还有桃子、核桃、酥油、奶渣、人参果、青稞酒等。茶和酒，装在核桃壳内。准备停当，主人把狗请来，很礼貌地说："舒服的狗，快乐的狗，请进餐吧！"如此三次，狗开始动嘴了。有些狗却乱吠乱叫，打翻盘子，掀倒茶酒，主人认为不吉利，于是把这种不识抬举的"贵宾"轰走。工布人认为狗吃什么，不吃什么，都是神的指使，因此全家诚惶诚恐，注视着狗的每一个动作。吃了糌粑或饼子，预示粮食丰产；吃了酥油或奶渣，预示牧业兴旺。千万不能吃肉，三十晚上狗吃肉，不死人也要闹瘟疫。奇怪的是，这天晚上，狗居然极少吃肉，也不知工布人采取了什么预防措施。

吃"结达"

狗吃饱了，人再吃团圆饭，围着火塘坐一圈，烤着暖烘烘的青冈柴火，喝青稞酒、酥油茶，吃一种特酥的食品——"结达"。结达是用酥油、牛奶调和面粉做成的面疙瘩，戳在尖尖的木棍上，

Eating "Jieda"

After dogs are full, people have family reunion meal, sit around fireplace, warm themselves by burning oriental white oak timbers, drink barley wine, ghee tea, and eat Jieda, a kind of special crisp food. Jieda is dough ball made of ghee, milk and flour and is toasted on sharp stick. People eat it after it has been toasted, and it is very delicious and appetizing.

伸到火里烤，烤熟一个吃
一个，味道特别好，特别
香。

People must have a big meal and eat their fill. It's said that night ghosts will come and carry people, if one doesn't eat his or her fill, he or she may be carried by ghosts because of light weight. He or she will not be carried by ghosts because he or she eats and drinks to his or her satisfaction. Therefore, eating up one's fill or not is a question of staying alive. It's very strange that ghosts are driven vigorously, and they come back to carry people, even precautions cannot ward off sudden attacks.

这天晚上是一定要
吃饱，拼命吃，胀得肚子
鼓鼓的。据说半夜鬼还要
进来背人，不吃饱，身子
骨轻飘飘的，说不定就被
鬼背跑了。吃饱喝足了，
鬼背不走。因此吃饱不吃
饱的问题，是生死存亡的
问题。叫人纳闷儿的是，
傍晚刚刚轰轰烈烈地赶完
鬼，半夜鬼又来背人，真
是防不胜防。

Carrying Water and Sacrificing to Harvest Goddess

背水，祭祀丰收女神

On the first day of New Year, Gongbo people will go out to fire powder shotgun to meet the coming of New Year when the cock crows for the first time. In the morning, housewives will carry water buckets and bring barley wine and "Cuo" (Zanba bun used for sacrifice) to carry water from water sources. Beside the river, they burn herbs and branches to call gods in smoke. On the way home, they cannot turn back and speak, because the first round of water is filled with "Yang" (good luck), and "Yang" will run to others' buckets if they turn back or speak.

大年初一，鸡叫头
遍，工布人都要出门，放
火药枪，迎接新的一年的
到来。这天早晨，主妇
们也要赶早起来背着水
桶，带着青稞酒和"措"
（祭祀用的糌粑团），到
水源处背水。在水边，煨
烧香草香树枝，让袅袅青
烟召唤神灵。在回家的路
上，不管遇到什么人，都
不能回头，不能讲话，因
为头轮水里装满了"央"
（福运），回头或讲话，

"央"就跑到别人的水桶里去了。

背回来头轮水，倒进神佛前的净水碗里，还用它拌糌粑做供果，兑青稞酒。在拉萨，初一清早，人们要到大昭寺朝拜释迦牟尼佛像；在工布，人们却是带上供品和青稞酒，来到自家最好的一块庄稼地里，祭祀丰收女神。他们是在地里竖一根长长的木杆或树枝，木杆上挂经幡，下绑一把麦草，麦草是丰收女神的宝座。搬一些石头，在木杆前搭个祭台，祭台上摆好各种供品，煨烧香草香树，意思是请统治田地的保护神来接受供养膜拜。农人用特殊的调子，这样高喊三次："洛雅阿妈！洛雅阿妈！洛雅阿妈！请用餐吧！请用餐吧！请用餐吧！"（"洛雅阿妈"意为丰收女神妈妈。）然后，他们围着祭台唱歌跳舞，娱乐丰收女神，请求她保佑庄稼丰收。

They carry the first round of water, pour it into clean water bowl in front of Buddha's image, and mix it with Zanba to make offerings and dilute barley wine. In Lhasa, people will go to the Jokhang Temple to worship the image of Sakyamuni; in Gongbo, people will bring offerings and barley wine to their best cropland and sacrifice to the Harvest Goddess. They erect a long wood pole or branch with pray flags at the top, and a bundle of ryegrass is tied at the bottom, which is the throne of the Harvest Goddess. They carry some stones to make a sacrificial altar before the wood pole, various kinds of offerings are placed on it, they burn ryegrass and tree branches, which means inviting the protective goddess dominating fields to accept offering and worship. Peasants shout three times in special tones, "Luoya Mother! Luoya Mother! Luoya Mother! Please dine! Please dine! Please dine!" ("Luoya Mother" means the Harvest Goddess) Then, they sing and dance around the sacrificial altar, entertain the Harvest Goddess and pray for harvest of crops.

3 藏北安多藏区的新年
New Year of Amdo Tibetan Region in North Tibet

Amdo Tibetan region in north Tibet is located in Qiangtang Plateau, and is the high-mountain gorge area neighboring Qinghai, Gansu, Sichuan and Tibet. There are millions of Tibetans in this broad area, and the Tibetans here celebrate New Year on the first day of the first month like Lhasa.

On the morning of the first day of Amdo Tibetan region in north Tibet, people get up early. It's said that goddess on the heaven will come out to see which is the earliest family getting up, and she will bring good luck to them; there is another saying that the earliest family will have good luck in New Year. Generally speaking, housewives get up early, they fire and boil tea after getting up, and then their family members get up. The first thing is to go to "Laze" to erect arrow mount, burn incense and sacrifice to gods. Persons coming late just add

藏北安多藏区位于羌塘高原，介于青海、甘肃、四川与西藏接壤的高山峡谷地带。在这广袤的空间，生存着数以万计藏族人，这里的藏人也和拉萨地区一样是以正月初一为新年。

藏北的安多藏区的初一早晨，人们很早就起床。一说是天上的女神要出来看，谁家起得最早就给谁家降吉祥；另一说是起得最早的人家在新的一年会碰上好运气。一般来说，起得最早的是家庭主妇，她们首先起床生火、烧茶，然后家人才起来。起来的第一件事就是去

"拉则"插箭垛煨桑祭神。后到的人只是在已经燃起的煨桑堆上加松枝、柏枝、桑面（糌粑）等物，献酒浆，跪拜叩首，添箭杆。第一个人燃起桑烟后，便向四周吹吉祥的海螺，海螺以白色为佳。有的还放鞭炮，给神壮声威，制造隆重气氛。远近山头都有桑烟燃起，各家各户的桑炉里都腾起了桑烟，举目四望，都是或淡或浓的桑烟。祭毕，人们各自回家吃早饭。家里人互相拜年道贺，儿子拜父母，晚辈拜长辈。吃完早饭，再去给村里年长者或辈分高的人拜年，或是到寺庙磕头、转经。由此看来，藏北安多藏区的初一是不像拉萨地区那样在新年初一只是在家中与家人团聚而不出门。

在安多藏区的很多地方，大年初一禁止扫地，也不背水、挑水；而不像在拉萨等地区，家庭主妇大年初一的第一件事就是要去泉边或者井旁打来第一桶水，喂饱牲畜。

安多藏区的年节，还

pine and cypress branches, Sang flour (Zanba) etc., offer wine, kneel, kowtow and add arrow shafts. After the first person burns incense, he or she blows auspicious conch to all directions, and the white conch is the best. Some people set off firecrackers, uphold reputation of gods, and create grand atmosphere. There is smoke burnt from near and far hills, and incenses are burnt in burners of households. If people look around, they will see light or heavy smoke everywhere. After sacrifice, people will return home to have breakfast. Family members congratulate mutually, sons say Happy New Year to parents and the junior says Happy New Year to the senior. After breakfast, they pay New Year calls to the senior or persons in higher ranks in villages, or go to temples to kowtow and pray. Therefore, the first day of Amdo Tibetan region in north Tibet is not like that of Lhasa, where people don't go out, but stay at home to get together with family members.

In many places in Amdo Tibetan region, sweeping floor and carrying water are forbidden on the first day of New Year; unlike Lhasa, the first thing of housewives on the first day is to carry the first bucket of water from spring or well and feed domestic animals.

There are new conventions of New Year celebration

in Amdo Tibetan region. Men (or old men at home) get up in the morning, they run to lair or sheep pen to see sleeping posture of ox and sheep, any direction of ox and sheep's sleeping posture will mean that the coming year will be auspicious, three-colored and five-colored cloths are hung on head of ox, then ox and sheep are driven to walk towards the direction. "Buxin" is an interesting activity, and it links with agricultural production closely. As for young men and women, saying good luck one another in New Year is the first round to develop friendships.

有出新的习惯。清晨男人们（或家里的老人们）一起来，就往牛圈或羊圈里跑，去看牛羊的卧法，牛羊的头朝东南西北四方的任何一方，将意味着来年这个方向是吉祥的，于是给牛的头上、身上拴挂三色、五色花布后赶着牛羊向此方向走几步。步新是一个非常有趣的活动，它与农业生产紧密相连，而对青年男女来说，正是年节中相互道声吉祥，联络情感的第一回合。

4 昌都地区藏历新年
Tibetan New Year of Qamdo Prefecture

昌都地处藏东三江流域，人杰地灵，民风粗犷。男子素有"康巴汉子"美誉，女性温柔善良。昌都一带风俗与其他地区差异较大，从他们过藏历年的风俗里面可以看到一些。

过年前的准备工作与拉萨和日喀则相似，清扫房屋，制作食品，绘吉祥图案，吃"古吐"等，但昌都一带过年，家家必须炖牛头或羊头。人们常说："藏族过年吃牛头，汉族过年放鞭炮。"认为过年不吃牛头羊头，等于没有过年。

大年初一，全家老

Qamdo Prefecture is located in Three Rivers Watershed, it is a beautiful place with talented people and boorish custom. Men are called "Kangba men" and women are gentle and kind. The conventions in Qamdo differ from other areas, which can be seen from their conventions to celebrate Tibetan New Year.

Preparatory works before celebrating New Year are similar to those of Lhasa and Shigatse, they clean houses, make foods, draw auspicious pattern, eat "Gutu" etc., but households in Qamdo must stew ox head or sheep head when New Year is celebrated. People often say, "Tibetans eat ox head for New Year, and Han people set off firecrackers." They think that New Year celebration without ox head or sheep head means nothing.

On the first day of New Year, all family members

get up early, and old men go into Buddhist Prayer Room to burn incense, sacrifice and worship. Young men and women carry water buckets to carry the first bucket of holly water from river, spring or stream. People coming to river burn incenses at first, throw five cereals, "Suzan" (which is powder mixed with ghee and Zanba and is specially used to burn and sacrifice to gods and dead people) and so on, worship God of New Year, and pray for good luck and health for all living beings.

When having breakfast on the first day of New Year, all family members wear new clothes, sit according to seniority, housewife holds Qiema box with both hands, and wish the whole family "Tashi Delek" in New Year. People hold "Qiema" among thumb, index finger and middle finger, and throw it to the sky three times, dip ring finger into bowl when offering wine and tea and flip it to the sky three times, which shows worshiping the three treasures of Buddhism or heaven, earth and celestial beings. Young people offer Hadas to the senior and wish them longevity, and the senior gives Hadas in return and hope that everything is fine and they have successful career. After mutual blessing, they have breakfast including Zanba, ghee, milk residue, cake, fruit, ginseng fruit, beef and mutton and so on. Family members get together and will not visit guests on this day generally. Relatives and good friends pay New Year calls and offer Hadas mutually on the second day.

小一大早起床，当雄鸡初鸣后，老年人进佛堂，烧香供祭，磕头礼佛。青年男女背上水桶到河边、泉水或溪水边争抢新年第一桶圣水。到河边的人，先煨桑，在桑烟中撒五谷、"苏糌"（酥油、糌粑合拌的粉专门用来焚烧、祭神、祭亡灵）等，敬新年之神，并祈祷世上所有的生灵吉祥安康。

初一早餐时，一家人穿好新装，按辈就座，家庭主妇双手举起切玛盒，祝全家新年"扎西德勒"。用拇指、食指和中指捏"切玛"向空中撒三下，敬酒、敬茶用无名指在碗中蘸一下，向空中弹三次，表示敬奉三宝或天地神灵。年轻人给长辈献哈达祝福长寿，长辈回敬年轻人万事大吉，事业有成。相互祝福后，享用早餐糌粑、酥油、奶渣、饼子、果子、人参果、牛羊肉等。初一这一天，一般为家人欢聚，互不走访。初二亲朋好友相互拜年，敬献哈达。

初三是超佛日。人们穿上最华丽、昂贵的盛装，佩戴各种珍贵的饰品（九眼珠、红珊瑚、金银首饰、护身盒、银刀等）。早餐后，手捧哈达、藏香、熬好的酥油、柏树枝、果子等，成群结队涌向朝佛路上。一边煨桑，一边转寺院，借此机会互相展示服饰。此时人们会议论，谁的衣服最华丽、昂贵，谁佩戴的饰品价值高；哪家的小伙子英俊潇洒，哪家的姑娘漂亮迷人等。转完寺院后，人们纷纷来到寺院内各大小神殿献哈达，为酥油灯添油，为家中去世的人布施，焚烧写有逝者名字的纸片，给乞丐发放食物或钱财。

在农村牧区，部分群众到寺院转经朝佛，多数人要到神山祭山神。人们把马具装饰一新，驮上丰盛的饮食，穿好盛装，佩戴护身盒、长刀、藏式火药枪，如同出征一般，骑马奔驰到自己所崇拜的神山集会。先在山顶的嘛呢石堆山竖起五颜六色

The third day is the transcending Buddha day. People wear the most splendid and expensive clothes and various kinds of precious ornaments (Nine-eyed gem, red coral, gold and silver jewels, protective box and silver knife etc.) After breakfast, people carry Hadas, Tibetan incenses, stewed ghee, cypress branches, fruits etc. with hands, and rush towards pilgrimage road in groups. They burn incenses, visit temples and take the chance to display clothes and ornaments. Meanwhile, people will discuss about whose clothes are the most splendid and expensive, whose ornaments are the most valuable, which young man is handsome and which young woman is beautiful and charming and so on. After visiting temples, people come to big and small shrines to offer Hadas, add oil into ghee lamps, sacrifice to the dead of family, burn papers with names of the dead, and distribute foods or money to beggars.

In rural pastoral areas, some common people visit temples to worship Buddhas, and most people will go to Holly Mountain to sacrifice to Mountain God. People decorate harnesses newly, carry plenty of foods and drinks, dress up, carry protective box, long knife and Tibetan powder shotgun, ride horses, and run to their worshipped Holly Mountain for assembly like an expedition. They erect colorful pray flags at the top of Mount Mani piled by stones, burn incenses, make offerings, throw five cereals and "Longda" (wind-horse flags) to the sky, and wish good luck and success. They fire powder shotgun, shout "Lajialuo" (meaning god's victory) loudly, chant Mani scriptures and pray blessing to Mountain God.

On the third day, either urban or rural residents worshiping Buddhas and visiting temples, or peasants, herdsmen and common people climbing mountain and sacrificing to Mountain God get together in streets and lanes spontaneously in the afternoon, or in lanes in agricultural and pastoral areas, they drink barley wine and dance. Residents in Qamdo towns like dancing wild and enthusiastic Guozhuang; common people in Mangkang and Zuogong like dancing beautiful and smooth Xuanzi; and people in Tengchen and Riwoche etc. like "Zhuo dance" and Reba dance of pastoral area.

On the fourth day, relatives and good friends begin to pay New Year calls till the fifteenth day of the first month.

的经幡，煨大堆桑火，供祭品，向天空抛撒五谷和"龙达"（风马旗）祝福运气亨通。鸣放火药枪，放开嗓门高声吼"拉加罗"（意为神胜利），诵嘛呢经，并祈祷山神的保佑。

初三这天，不管是朝佛转寺院的城乡居民，还是转山祭山神的农牧民群众，到下午都会自发地聚集在大街小巷，农牧区则在草坪上，一边喝青稞酒，一边跳舞。昌都城镇的居民喜欢跳粗犷奔放的锅庄；芒康、左贡一带的群众喜欢跳轻柔优美的弦子；丁青、类乌齐等地的人们则喜欢跳牧区"卓舞"和热巴舞。

初四开始亲朋好友相互拜年，直到正月十五。

5 阿坝藏区新年
New Year of Aba Tibetan Region

阿坝藏区地处四川省与西藏自治区交界的横断山脉，现名为阿坝藏族自治州。由于地处交通要道，多民族杂居于此，因此阿坝藏区的新年呈现出多种文化的格局。

阿坝的藏族，可分为草地藏族和嘉绒藏族，其年节以这两地藏族最为典型。

一、草地藏族的年节

草地藏族的年节也是在每年农历正月初举行，为期一个星期左右。节日前，每家每户都要打扫卫生，并按照当地习惯，

Aba Tibetan region is bounded on the transverse Mountains between Sichuan Province and Tibet Autonomous Region, and is called Aba Tibetan Region Autonomous Prefecture. Because it is located in main arteries of traffic, many minorities live here, so New Year of Aba Tibetan region presents pattern of multiple cultures.

Aba Tibetans can be divided into Caodi Tibetans and Jiarong Tibetans, and New Year Festival is characterized by Tibetans in these two places.

1. New Year Festival of Caodi Tibetans

Caodi Tibetans also celebrate New Year Festival in lunar January each year, which lasts about one week. Before the festival, each household will clean, and pour waste water and wastes to the west when the sun sets according to the local convention, which symbolizes that all unlucky and unhealthy things will disappear with the sunset. Then households brew barley wine, make oil and milk cakes, prepare festival foods such as blood sausage, fresh milk, boiled meat and so on. On the first day of New Year, hostesses of households must get up before daybreak, take buckets to river and well to carry water, which will be mixed with fresh milk and used for the whole family to wash faces and hands. After combing and washing, family members play "dragon lamps", burn incenses pleasantly and hope that they will have bumper water and grass and fat domestic animals, and the whole family have meal together. Before dining, everyone must eat a little bit of Zanba flour, and show that they are people eating Zanba and will not forget ancestors.

People in villages will not go out in the first three days of New Year and they get together to watch "dance for gods", i.e. "Qiangmu" which I have introduced previously. Moreover, men and women sing and dance happily with rhythms of music instruments such as drum, flute, *erhu* and so on. Three days later, people help the aged and lead the young to visit villagers, and pay New Year calls and congratulate mutually.

According to the local convention, girls and

在太阳快要下山时，将污水、赃物一律往西边倒掉，表示让一切不吉利、不利于人们身体健康的东西随日落而消失。然后各家酿青稞酒，做油饼、奶饼，准备血肠、肉肠、鲜奶和手抓肉等节日食品。大年初一，家家户户的女主人必须在天刚亮时起床，带上水桶到河边、井池背水，背回来的水，要放一些鲜奶子，用这种水给全家人洗脸洗手。梳洗完毕，大家兴致勃勃地玩"龙灯"，烧柏香，祝愿当年水草丰茂，牲畜肥壮，接着全家聚餐。饭前，每人必须先吃点糌粑面，表示自己是吃糌粑的人，不忘祖宗。

此地新年的头三天，村寨里的人一般不外出，大家聚集在一起观看"跳神"，即前面介绍过的"羌姆"。另外，男女青年则欢天喜地地随着锣鼓、笛子、二胡等乐器的节拍歌舞。三天后，人们扶老携幼，走村串寨，彼此登门拜年祝贺。

按照当地传统习俗，

节日期间，姑娘们和大嫂经常结伴"抢"男子的东西吃，男人们不得表示任何不满和反抗。有的村寨的青壮年还展开"奔牛"活动，比赛时，两人相距两米左右，抬一条牦牛绳；中间作一个标记，谁将对方拉过标线为胜。夜间，村寨男女多聚集在村外，欢歌喜跳。

二、嘉绒藏区的年节

嘉绒藏族主要分布在大小金川流域，自称嘉绒娃。他们依地区不同而称呼各异，如汶川原瓦寺土司所属嘉绒藏族，自称为德布利，四土的则自称为"垄巴"或"垄巴布"，理县五屯的则自称为"喜卡布"，等等，因而在嘉绒藏族中，年节文化也各放异彩。

在嘉绒藏族聚居的土司区，每年的十月十三和冬月十三要过糌粑年。早晨吃糌粑茶、肉，休息一天。第二天用荞面包糌粑肉包。第三天，也吃糌粑（平时不吃）；熬茶，一

young women often "seize" things from men to eat, and men shall not show any discontent and resistance. Some young men in villages hold "Bull-running" activity. During race, the distance of two persons is about two meters, they carry a yak rope with a mark in the middle, and the person who pulls the other to the mark is the winner. At night, men and women get together outside villages, sing and dance happily.

2. New Year Festival of Jiarong Tibetan Region

Jiarong Tibetans are mainly distributed in big and small Jinchuan River valley, and call themselves Jiarong people. Names differ according to regions, for example, the original Wasi Chieftain of Wenchuan was Jiarong Tibetan, and it called itself Debuli, Situ calls itself "Longba" or "Longbabu", Wutun calls itself "Xikabu" etc., so Jiarong Tibetans have colorful New Year Festival cultures.

Zaban Festivals are held on October 13th and November 13th in chieftain regions of Jiarong Tibetans each year. They have Zanba tea and meat in the morning and take a day off. They make Zanba meat buns with buckwheat on the second day. On the third day, they also eat Zanba (they don't eat it at normal times); and they make tea without ghee usually. They eat cold steamed dumplings and flat bread. They offer sheep, burn incenses and offer sacrifices to tombs.

Dangba celebrates New Year on November 13th and sacrifices to "Amei Rige" Gods, and it's said they are a man and a woman. They make long buns, whose number is equal to the number of men. Double horns are made at the top of buns on the evening of the thirteenth day, and images of gods including "Amei Rige" are hung on the kitchen wall with coarse flour, and long horn buns are placed on plates to sacrifice to gods. They prepare wine and flour, fire a brazier with cypress branches covered by buns, throw flour and pig fat, and family head kneels in front of images of gods to pray and hope that the whole family members are safe and sound, domestic animals are healthy and vigorous, and crops are bumper. Then they will drink wine for four days and eat pig fat, buns and Za wine. They don't go out and invite guests.

Xiaojin Tibetans celebrate New Year on November 13th. It was said that evil ghosts (Silunbu) ate people. An old woman had a son, and he can eat and talk three days after his birth. His mother cannot afford him because he ate too much, and he was sent to forests to hunt wild animals. When he grew up, he had the strongest power, killed the evil ghost, common people wanted to elect him as a king, and the king wanted to abdicate and hand over power to him, but he refused and continued to be common people, eliminated evils and made contribution

般没有酥油；并且还吃冷烧卖面饼。第四、五天，送羊，熏烟祭坟。

党坝十一月十三也过年，敬奉"阿美日各"神，据说此神是一男一女。十三日晚做长馋馋，其数目依家中男子人数而定，馋馋上顶做双角，十三日早晨用连麸面在灶房墙上画"阿美日各"诸神像，把长角馍馍放在盘内敬神。另设酒、面，生一火盆，架上柏枝，枝上放馍，并撒一些面，一点猪朥，由当家人跪在神像前祷告一家老少平安、牲畜健旺、庄稼丰收。然后喝四天酒，吃猪朥、馍馍，咂酒。不出门，不请客。

小金藏族冬月十三也过年。据说古时恶鬼（斯仑布）吃人，有一老妇生有一子，出生三天后能吃能说。后来吃得多了，养不起，就送到山林中去捕食野兽。此孩长大后，力大无比，打死了恶鬼，群众要选他为王，国王也让位给他，他不肯，还是老老实实做自己的平民，为百姓除害造福。因此，每月十二日晚、十三日晚，家家以面做羊头，家里有几人就做几个，十二日晚打扫厨房卫生后供在厨房内，另以面印日月星形，放置酒内。到第二天早晨太阳升起的时候，各家在房顶熏烟祭奠这位英雄。在嘉绒的宅垄、汗牛、丹巴等地，都在冬月十三过年，纪念他，并且在纪念时还专门念一种经文。

三、白马藏人的年节庆祝

白马藏人也是藏族里比较特殊的一支，全族大概一万余人，分散居住在川甘交界处的四川省平武县、南坪县和甘肃省文县。其中平武县白马乡和甘肃文县铁楼乡是最大的聚居区。虽然同为藏族，但从他们的历史、地域、语言、服饰、习俗、信仰等方面看，他们同四川和西藏的藏族都有些差别。

白马藏人的祭祀年节活动很多，其中最隆重

to the mass. Therefore, households make sheep heads with flour on the evenings of the twelfth day and the thirteenth day every month, the number of sheep heads is equal to the number of family members, people clean kitchen on the evening of the twelfth day and offer sheep heads in kitchen, and they make the sun, the moon and the star shapes with flour and immerse them in wine. When the sun rises in the morning next day, households burn incenses on roofs to memorize this hero. The places including Zhailong, Hanniu and Danba etc. in Jiarong celebrate New Year on November 13th to commemorate him, and they chant a kind of scripture when commemorating him.

3. New Year Festival Celebration of Baima Tibetans

Baima Tibetan is a special branch among Tibetans, the whole clan has about ten thousand people, and they live on the border of Sichuan and Gansu, including Pingwu County and Nanping County of Sichuan Province and Wen County of Gansu Province. Baima Village of Pingwu County, Tielou Village of Wen County of Gansu Province are the largest inhabited regions. Although they are Tibetans, they differ from Tibetans in Sichuan and Tibet in terms of history, territory, language, clothes, conventions, religions and so on.

There are many New Year Festival sacrifice activities, among which Spring Festival is the grandest. On the eve of Spring Festival, Baima Tibetans celebrate Lantern Festival; on the first day of Spring Festival, they sacrifice to Fire God and the ceremony of "water offering" is held; poles are erected on the third day and the fourth day; wizards are invited to chant scriptures in the evening of the fifth day; and Caogai is danced to dispel disasters and bring good luck on the sixth day.

Dancing Caogai is the most attractive folk event among New Year celebration activities of Baima Tibetans, and has heavy primitive characteristics and ethnic features. "Caogai" is the transliteration of Baima Tibetan and means "mask". "Caogai dance" is dancing with masks to sacrifice to gods and ghosts, dispel disasters and pray. Comparing with popular "Qiangmu" in other Tibetan areas which has been introduced previously, Caogai dance of Baima people is similar to it in many aspects, but there are great differences between them.

Ceremony of dancing Caogai is held on the sixth day of the first month in the places such as Baima Village of Pingwu County. On the evening of the fifth day, people build sacrifice canopy in open field outside the village, there is a stack of fire in the middle of the sacrifice canopy, and wizards sit around the middle of the fire stack and chant scriptures. On the morning of the sixth day, people wearing five-colored gowns and white felt hats with white chicken feather bring prepared offerings to the fire stack when day breaks. Firstly, people

的就是春节。白马藏人在除夕之夜，欢闹元宵；大年初一，举行敬火神和作"贡水"仪式；初三、初四架杆；初五晚上请巫师念经；初六跳曹盖，驱灾纳吉。

跳曹盖是白马藏人年节活动中最为引人注目的民俗事项，具有浓郁的原始特点和民族特色。"曹盖"是白马藏语的音译，意为"面具"。"跳曹盖"即戴着面具跳祭祀神鬼的、驱灾祈福的舞蹈。和前面介绍过的其他藏区流行的"羌姆"相比，白马人的曹盖舞或许有异曲同工之处，但是也有很不相同的地方。

在平武县白马乡等地，跳曹盖的仪式是在每年正月初六举行。初五晚上，人们便在寨外空坝上搭上祭棚，在祭棚中间烧起一堆篝火，巫师们围在火堆旁念经。初六清晨，当东方刚刚发白的时候，穿五彩长袍，头戴插有雪白鸡毛的白色毡帽的人们，带着事先准备好的祭品来到火堆旁。首先，人们在巫师主持下，杀牛祭神。然后，跳"曹盖"的青壮年戴上巨大的木制面具，手持大刀锯子等舞具，围着火堆跳起了粗犷、古朴、刚健的曹盖舞。跳曹盖舞者至少三人，尽管头戴面具，在"咚咚咚"的鼓声和"哐哐哐"的锣声伴奏下，他们仍激烈地跳跃。舞蹈以手上动作为主，内容主要是模仿老熊等猛兽的动作，力争凶猛怪诞。接下来，跳至高潮时，还要从火堆上飞身纵过。每至此时，鼓锣齐鸣，群情振奋，然是壮观。接下来，跳曹盖的队伍围着寨子挨家挨户去跳。最后跳到田边地脚为止。据说，这是为了驱鬼，将鬼怪赶出寨外，保一年人畜平安、五谷丰登。

有研究显示，白马藏人的跳曹盖习俗是一种傩祭仪式，它的功能和目的主要是驱凶求吉，当然在过年的时候进行还有娱乐功能。在跳曹盖之前，要祭祀神灵，酬神的目的是

kill ox to sacrifice to gods under the direction of wizards. Then young men dancing "Caogai" wear giant wooden masks, hold props such as big knives and saws etc., and dance wild, simple and powerful Caogai around the fire stack. There are three Caogai dancers at least, they dance and jump to the accompaniment of drums and gongs although they wear masks. The dance focuses on hand movements, and contents mainly include imitating actions of violent animals such as old bear and try to be ferocious and weird. Next, they will jump from the fire stack in the climax. At this moment, drums and gongs are played together and people become excited. What a splendid view it is! Next, team dancing Caogai comes to each household to perform around the village till fields and boards of villages finally. It's said that it can drive ghosts out of the village and hopes that people and animals are safe and sound, and there is a good harvest.

Some studies show that the convention of dancing Caogai by Baima Tibetans is a kind of ritual ceremony, its function and purpose are mainly to dispel evils and pray for good luck, and it has the function of entertainment during New Year as well. Before dancing Caogai, people will sacrifice to holly spirits, and the purpose of rewarding gods is to invite them to drive disasters and offer blessings. Dancing Caogai is a kind of imitating and ceremonial dance with strong totem worship. Baima Tibetans worship boldness and power of bear, so they sacrifice to Black Bear God. Masks of Caogai dance are images of bear, and dance movements are mainly action imitating bear.

Mask for Caogai dance of Baima Tibetans is very characteristic, is made of local birch, and is usually as long as about 40 centimeters, as wide as 30 centimeters, the thickness of the top is two or three centimeters, that of the surface is one or two centimeters, it is large and thick, and its weight is over ten *jin*. Mask images are animals, mainly bear head, and Baima Tibetans called them "Dana Sijie". "Na" means "black", "Da" means "bear", "Sijie" means "holy spirits", and "Dana Sijie" means Black Bear God. Baima people believe in Black Bear God and think that it is the fiercest holly spirit which frightens ghosts, so they make mask into image of bear head and believe that it can drive ghosts and dispel plague. These masks are carved fiercely, showing their teeth, and frightening people. Two snakes twine on foreheads of some masks, or there are several heads, or a pair of sheep's horns, or an ox's tail, which is strange and simple. According to Baima Tibetans, fiercer mask images can frighten people strong. Masks are colorful, have diversified ornaments, some of them have their hair dishevelled or have beard or are tied with colorful ornaments, which have various kinds of forms or pure and

请神驱灾和降福。跳曹盖是一种模仿性的舞蹈，是带着浓厚图腾意味的仪式舞蹈。白马藏人崇拜熊的勇猛和强大，因此奉祀黑熊神，曹盖舞面具便是熊头形象，舞蹈动作也主要模仿熊的动作。

白马藏人跳曹盖舞时所戴的面具也非常有特色，是由当地所产桦木雕刻而成的，一般长约40厘米，宽约30厘米，顶部木厚2至3厘米，面部木厚1至2厘米，既大且厚，重约10多斤。其面具形象皆为动物，主要是熊头面具，白马藏人称为"达纳尸界"。"纳"是"黑"之意，"达"即指"熊"，"尸界"指"神灵"，"达纳尸界"即黑熊神。白马人崇奉黑熊神，认为它是鬼怪们最惧怕的神灵，故将面具做成熊头的形象，相信这样便能驱鬼逐疫。这些面具，一般都雕刻得凶猛异常，龇牙咧嘴，让人看了害怕。有的面具额头上有双蛇盘绕，或并列几个头，或配有一对羊角，或插有一条牛尾，奇异古朴。据白马藏人说：面具的形象，做得越凶狠，越让人害怕，就越好。面具色彩鲜艳斑斓，装饰多样，或披以散发，或贴有胡子，或绑以彩扎造型多样，线条古朴而稚拙。跳曹盖者除了佩戴这凶猛可怕的面具外，浑身着长毛衣服，五彩斑斓，平添几分"兽气"。跳曹盖的面具，平时挂在家里大门上方，驱邪纳吉，保一家平安，这颇似汉族信仰中门神的职责。

在整个的西南少数民族地区，火把节是一个非常传统的节日，也流行在多个少数民族当中。大家所熟知的彝族火把节不仅年年盛大壮观，而且被彝族视为新年的开始。而白马藏族与彝族、羌族等民族相处一地，因此火把节在他们的年节庆典当中也是十分重要的一环。

在每年正月十五日晚上，白马山寨的男女老少排着火把的长龙，一路高呼着，弯弯曲曲地穿过山寨，走遍田野地脚，

innocent designs. Caogai dancers wear fierce and terrible masks, clothes with long hair, which are colorful and add a sense of beant. Masks for Caogai dance are hung at the top of the gate of the house to dispel evils and bring good luck, bless family with safety, which function like duties of Door God in Han people's belief.

In the whole southwest area inhabited by ethnic minorities, Torch Festival is a traditional festival and is popular among many minority people. The well-known Torch Festival of Yi people is grand and splendid, and is regarded as the beginning of New Year by Yi people. Baima Tibetans live with Yi and Qiang people, so Torch Festival is an important part of their New Year Festival celebration.

On the evening of the fifteenth day of the first month each year, all people in Baima Village cross the village in long torch lines, go over fields, they use torches to dispel evils and pray good luck and happiness. In Baima Village, people pay particular attention to firing of the first torch, and they elect the oldest Ani (grandfather in Baima Tibetan) according to zodiac titles of lunar year. By that time, the old Ani fires torch firstly and leads the team to run, the latter one fires torch from the former one in turn and follows closely. They run and shout loudly, "Oh! Fire!" If two villages are adjacent, two teams of torches often approach towards the middle, they mix parallel and make into a circle, people sing and dance in the middle happily.

Tibetans in Mianning of Sichuan are very strange, it's said that they don't celebrate New Year in the first month, but New Year Festival is held in the middle of lunar June each year. Torch Festival in June is regarded as New Year Festival. As for Torch Festival, it was said that a man turned into an untamed dragon in the middle of June, and the dragon turned the land surrounded by four mountains into sea. In order to protect the land, people began to drive the untamed dragon, they held torches to drive it when it was dark, and they drove it to Guan County at last and tied it in Double-king Temple. Because they feared that it will make trouble, they decided to drive it once a year and killed livestock for sacrifice. Year after year, it has evolved into today's Torch Festival.

他们要用火把驱逐邪气，祈求吉祥和幸福。在白马山寨，点燃第一支火把很有讲究，要依照农历年号属相，推举最年长的阿尼（爷爷——白马藏语）承担。届时，老阿尼最先点燃火把，在前面带队小跑，后面的依次从前一个手中点燃火把紧跟着。众人一边跑，一边高喊："喔一把。"若是两寨相邻，两对火把往往向中间靠拢，并行糅杂，然后旋成一圈儿，人们就在中间载歌载舞，欢呼雀跃。

四川冕宁的藏族比较奇怪，据说他们正月不过新年，而年节是每年农历六月中旬举行。每年六月的火把节就被视为过年节。关于火把节的来历当地的说法是：以前有个人六月中旬变成了逆龙，并要把四山环绕之地变成大海。为了保地，大家就从早晨开始追赶逆龙，赶到天黑时就打着火把赶，最后把逆龙赶到了灌县，并把它拴在了二王庙下。因为怕它再作怪，便决定每年赶一次，而且一定要杀牲见血。这样年复一年，演变成现今的火把节。

火把节期间，以村寨为单位杀牛羊祭祀火神。入夜全寨的人都将自己准备的火把点燃，扔到村寨中心的晒场上，霎时间，火光冲天，十分壮观。年轻人把节前收集筛选好的朽木粉末撒到火把堆上，玩起"耍火把"的游戏。青年男女在火把节之夜对歌，跳舞，娱乐狂欢，通宵达旦。

也有传说最早的火把节是人们点起火把到庄稼地转悠，烧死庄稼地里的虫害，使来年农业得到好的收成。随着时间的推移，古老的火把节便成了人们向火神祈求丰收的传统节日。直到现在，点火把灭虫和蚊子，仍然是冕宁藏族防治农业病虫害和预防疾病行之有效的方法。

During Torch Festival, cattle and sheep are sacrificed to Fire God in unit of village. At night, all villagers fire their prepared torches, throw them to the dry field of the village, then flame roars in an instant, which is so splendid. Young men throw deadwood powder collected and selected before the festival onto the fire stack, and play the game of "playing torch". Young men and women sing in antiphonal style, dance and entertain at the night of Torch Festival, and the revelry continues all night.

It was also said that people strolled with torches to burn insect pests on crop lands to make a good harvest in coming year in the earliest Torch Festival. As time goes on, the ancient Torch Festival has become the traditional festival of people to pray to Fire God for harvest. Till now, firing torches to kill insects and mosquitoes is still the effective method for Mianning Tibetans to prevent agricultural insect pest and diseases.

6 青海玉树藏历年赛牦牛

Yak Racing for Tibetan New Year in Qinghai Yushu

Qinghai Yushu Tibetan Autonomous Prefecture holds special yak racing activity during Tibetan New Year. This kind of activity brings happy atmosphere to local Tibetan New Year particularly. Yak is divided into wild yak and domestic yak. Although domestic yaks have been domesticated for a long time, yaks which can be ridden have to be trained regularly. A wooden ring is worn on yak's nose, one end of the rein is tied on the ring, and the other is grasped in hands of rider. This kind of yak is powerful, good at walking, wild and violent, desires to excel over others, can fight on race field, and doesn't like other stable and slow yaks. However, some yaks are obedient and good at running, but don't run at all in the race field when seeing many people and act out of character, even run around all over the place, their stubborn temper makes audience laugh.

青海玉树藏族自治州在藏历年期间要举行别开生面的赛牦牛活动，这种活动给当地的藏历年带来了特别热烈欢乐的气氛。牦牛有野牦牛和家牦牛之分。家牦牛虽然是驯化很久的了，但能骑的牦牛还得在平时训练。鼻子上穿有木制的牛鼻圈，缰绳的一端系在牛鼻圈上，另一端则握在骑者手里。这种牛力大善走，剽悍性烈，争强好胜，在赛场上能冲锋陷阵，而不像其他的牛那样四平八稳，慢慢吞吞的。但是有的牛平时听话善跑，而到赛场上一见人多，便一反常态，打死也不跑一步，甚至左右乱窜，那倔犟的牛脾气惹得观众大笑不止。

骑手们对参加比赛的牦牛都非常喜爱，平时精心照料，加喂青稞料等。比赛那天，牛角上裹扎着绫绸，尾巴上系饰有花布条，背上还披盖着鲜丽的毛毯。骑手身穿氆氇褐衫，头戴狐皮帽，足登高靴，腰佩宝刀等饰物，袒露右臂，手握牛鞭。他们先接受亲朋好友的祝福，饮酒三杯后，跨上牛背，勒缰举鞭，等待起跑令。锣鸣鼓响，鞭落缰弛，牦牛便如箭离弦，疾驰如风。观众齐声呐喊，骑手频频挥鞭。除了个别临阵畏缩的牛外，大多数牛都奋力前奔，直到终点。第一个到达终点的骑手备受人们尊敬，亲朋们纷纷上前祝贺，敬美酒、献哈达。如果在决赛中获得冠军，骑手就被视为英雄。人自豪，牛也身价倍增，往往有人愿出高价收买。

牦牛是藏族人珍爱的家畜，皮毛骨肉和役用都

Riders love all yaks participating in race, take good care of them, and feed them with barley. On the day of racing, silk damask is tied on yak's horns, colorful cloth strips are tied on tail, bright and beautiful blanket is covered on back. Riders wear brown Pulu shirts, fox fur hats, high boots, put treasured swords on their waists, expose right arm and hold whip in hand. They accept blessings of relatives and good friends firstly, drink three glasses of wine, mount on horse, rein up and hold whip, and wait for starting order. Gongs and drums are played, and riders lash yaks with whips, loosen reins, and ride fast. Audience shout in unison, and riders wave whips frequently. Except several yaks having cold feet, most yaks make efforts to run to the finishing point. The first rider reaching the finishing point wins a high reputation from people, relatives and friends come to congratulate him and offer fine wine and Hadas. If one wins the championship in the final, he is regarded as a hero. He feels honored and proud, the yak will become treasure, and people want to buy it at a high price.

Yak is a precious domestic animal of Tibetans, its hide, fur, bone, meat and ability to work are superior to other oxen. Therefore, this kind of domestic animal which is slow in normal times can be driven to race field by people, and it displays its graceful bearing and strives for honor. Tibetans in eastern Qinghai agricultural areas have the convention of playing yak dance in Spring Festival although they don't have conditions for yak racing. Yak acted by two persons has coiled corns, angry eyes, long hair, large hoofs, stubborn and violent characters, and vivid image.

优于其他牛类。因此，这种平时慢吞吞的牲畜被人们赶上赛场，展示风采，争取荣誉。青海东部农业区的藏族，春节时虽没有赛牦牛的条件，却有着扮演牦牛舞的习俗。双人扮演的牦牛、盘角怒目，毛长蹄大，倔犟性烈，形象逼真。

第五章
藏历年的传承与变迁

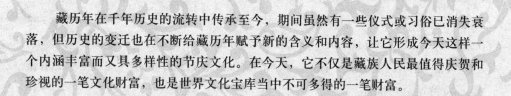

　　藏历年在千年历史的流转中传承至今，期间虽然有一些仪式或习俗已消失衰落，但历史的变迁也在不断给藏历年赋予新的含义和内容，让它形成今天这样一个内涵丰富而又具多样性的节庆文化。在今天，它不仅是藏族人民最值得庆贺和珍视的一笔文化财富，也是世界文化宝库当中不可多得的一笔财富。

Chapter Five

Inheritance and Transition of Tibetan New Year

Although some ceremonies or conventions have disappeared and decayed during the transition of Tibetan New Year having a history of one thousand years, the transition of history has endowed new implications and contents to Tibetan New Year constantly and made it such a diversified festival celebration culture with rich connotations. At present, it is a cultural wealth which Tibetans congratulate and cherish and is a rare wealth in treasury of world culture.

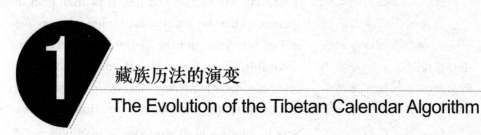

藏族历法的演变

The Evolution of the Tibetan Calendar Algorithm

As cultural heritages, cultural conventions of Tibetan New Year have been inherited by Tibetans for nearly one thousand years. This booklet aims at displaying cultural heritages with rich connotations to readers and letting more people share this unique cultural property. However, heritages can be inherited and transited, culture is not a static thing, and it changes constantly since its foundation. From the establishment of Tibetan New Year till today, we can feel the long process of its inheritance and changes and see different social and cultural factors being affected and integrated mutually in the long history from various kinds of forms of Tibetan New Year celebration.

从历史到现在，藏历年的文化习俗在近千年的流转中作为一份文化遗产被藏族人民传承至今。这本小册子旨在将这份内涵丰富的文化遗产展示给读者，让更多的人分享这份独特的文化财产。不过，遗产既有传承也会变迁，文化并不是静止不变的，从它诞生那天起它就不断在改变着。从藏历年的诞生到今天人们庆祝藏历年的种种形式，我们可以感受到它传承与改变的漫长过程，看到各种不同的社会文化因素在漫长的历史中是如何相互影响、相互交融的。

年节，从它最原本的含义来看，起初反映的都是民族生产生活中庆祝丰收和调节人们心态的集体聚会性活动。它举行的时间一般都在丰收之季，也即它是每个民族依据自己生存的时空物候变化所界定的一年的年末和下一年的年初。同时，它也反映了每个民族根据其生产生活在不断认识自然规律与自身文化的关系。

生活在青藏高原广袤土地上的藏族先民，依据其生产方式，最开始在农区就是以"麦熟为岁首"；在牧区就以牛羊最为肥壮的时候为年末和下一年的开始。所以，如今在藏区的很多地方，还流行两个节日，一个是"望果节"，一个是牧区的"赛马节"，据说都跟藏族最开始的纪年有关系。

"望果节"在夏历的七八月份，"望"是田地的意思，"果"是转圈，举行这个仪式活动时，人们围着丰收的麦田歌唱、跳舞，欢庆收获的喜悦。而当时又以"麦熟为

In terms of the most original meaning, New Year Festival reflects collectively gathering activities celebrating harvests and comforting people's mentality in national production and life. It is often held in seasons of harvest usually, each ethnic defines the end of last year and the beginning of next year according to spatio-temporal and phenological changes of their existence. Meanwhile, it also shows that each ethnic understands relations between laws of nature and its own culture according to its production and life.

Tibetan ancestors living on broad land of Qinghai-Tibet Plateau see the ripening of wheat as the beginning of a year in agricultural areas according to their production mode initially; and they see the time when cattle and sheep become fat in pastoral areas at the end of a year and the beginning of next year. Therefore, there are two popular festivals in many places in Tibetan areas, one is Ongkor Festival and the other is Horse Racing Festival, and it was said that they were related to the most initial calendar. Ongkor Festival is held in July and August in lunar calendar, "Ong" means field, "Kor" means circling, and people sing and dance around harvest wheat fields and celebrate happiness of harvest when they hold this ceremonial activity. At that time, people saw the ripening of wheat as the beginning of a year, so festival celebration at the end of a year in Tibetan culture engaging in agriculture is today's Ongkor Festival in the time of the ripening of wheat, which implies praying and celebration. Compared with activities of Ongkor Festival in pastoral areas, traditional pastoral areas also have Horse Racing Festival at the end of a year. Cattle and sheep are fat and strong in July and August in lunar calendar, so horse racing activity has been inherited as a festival celebrating harvest at the end of a year.

At present, Ongkor Festival and Horse Racing Festival are inherited generally in Tibetan areas, and the implication of celebrating harvests doesn't take changes. However, the function of celebration at the end of a year is less obvious than the previous function, hilarious scenes and significance as New Year Festival celebration have taken changes in the heart of common people. Festival being celebrated at the end of a year has been gradually transferred to other seasons, and it is the current Tibetan New Year. The formation of Tibetan New Year has very close relations with the establishment and improvement of the Tibetan calendar.

In the introduction of chapter one, we can see that the making and constant improvement of Tibetan calendar is the direct reason for the formation of Tibetan New Year. The Tibetan calendar was formed and adopted in 1027, and soon afterwards Tibetan New Year was formed. At that time, local authority

岁首", 因此从事农业的藏族文化中的年终节庆, 就是现在麦熟时季蕴含着祈求和庆贺意义的"望果节"。而相对于农区的"望果节"活动, 传统的牧区也有作为年终庆典的赛马节, 在夏历的七八月份, 牧区草原上的牛羊肥壮, 赛马活动就成为一年年末庆祝丰收的节日传承了下来。

而现在, "望果节"和赛马节在藏区普遍传承, 它原本庆祝丰收的含义并没有发生多大的改变。但是其岁末年终庆典的功能已没有以前那样明显, 而且热闹的场面和在民众心目中作为年节庆典的意义也发生改变。而作为年终庆典的节日渐渐转移到了别的时节上, 即现在的藏历年。而藏历年的诞生跟藏历的产生和完善有着非常紧密的关系。

在第一个章节的介绍中, 我们可以看到藏历的产生和不断完善是藏历年最终形成的直接原因。公元1027年, 藏历最终形成并开始使用, 由此不久,藏历年产生。当时西藏的地方政权规定了藏历年的时间和庆祝形式。由此，藏历年就逐渐取代了"望果节"和赛马节年终庆典的职能。

由此可见，节日庆典的含义是随着历史的发展而不断改变的。在藏历年的产生中间，政府推广的力量起了很大的作用。除了政府推广的力量，在漫长的历史过程当中，藏地文化与其他各族文化之间不断交流与融合，藏族文化吸收了不少其他民族的文化，并将它们与自身文化融合在一起形成一些独特的文化习俗。从人们过藏历年的习俗中可以窥见一斑，特别在藏族与其他族群杂居相处之地域，更能够看出藏历年习俗的改变以及各种文化如何交融。

譬如在青海和四川的藏区，很多地方是藏人跟汉人杂居在一起。他们的年节就明显受到汉文化很深的影响。在青海靠近西藏的玉树地区，藏人过藏历年的氛围还很浓重，可

stipulated time and celebration forms of the Tibetan New Year. Therefore, Tibetan New Year replaced the celebration function of Ongkor Festival and Horse Racing Festival at the end of a year.

It can be seen that implications of festival celebration can take changes with their developments in history constantly. In the formation of Tibetan New Year, the force of goverment promotion plays a great role. Besides the force of goverment promotion, culture in Tibetan areas communicates and is integrated with cultures of other ethnics in the long historical process. Tibetan culture has absorbed cultures of other ethnics, integrated them with it and formed some unique cultural conventions. It can be seen from conventions of celebrating Tibetan New Year and we can also see changes of conventions and integration methods with other cultures in regions where Tibetans and other clans inhabited.

For example, Tibetans live with Han people in Tibetan areas of Qinghai and Sichuan. Their New Year Festival is affected by Chinese culture greatly. The atmosphere of Tibetan New Year celebration in Yushu region near Qinghai is very strong, but some Tibetans in other regions of Qinghai celebrate Spring Festival, rather than Tibetan New Year; in terms of New Year celebration ceremonies, many places keep both Tibetan elements and obvious Han elements. For example, many places in Qinghai Tibetan region have the popular traditional Tibetan New Year celebration saying that family reunion meal shall be eaten as much as possible, because Yama will come to weigh people after they are full and pronounce blessings; on the fourteenth day and the fifteenth day of the first month, Tibetans around Qinghai Lake will go to Ta'er Temple and make a pilgrimage, and it can be seen that Buddhism is deeply rooted in the hearts of people; Tibetans in some places will make a pilgrimage to "Lashize" (meaning hilltop in Tibetan), and they can watch Han people's flower lantern exhibition and fire performance on the pilgrimage road and destination; it's said that Ghee Lantern Festival which is held in Tibetan areas on the fifteenth day of the first month each year is greatly affected by Lantern Festival of the Han ethnic region of China on the fifteenth day of the first month. In some Tibetan areas of Sichuan, antithetical couplets can be seen at gates of many Tibetan houses in New Year in order to bring good luck; and it's said that popular athletic activities in Tibetan areas during Tibetan New Year such as wrestling, casting stone and archery etc. are greatly influenced by Mongolian culture. Therefore, the constant integration with foreign cultures is also the important factor of the transition of Tibetan New Year conventions.

是在青海其他地区的一些藏族已不过藏历年，而是过普遍的春节；从过年的仪式来看，很多地方是既保留有藏族的元素，而又有明显的汉族元素。例如青海藏区的很多地方还是流传年夜饭要尽量多吃的习俗，因为吃饱后阎王要来称体重赐新一年的福，这是一个很传统的藏族过年时的说法；正月十四、十五，青海环湖一带藏族要到塔尔寺去朝拜，可见佛教思想在民间根深蒂固；有些地方是要到山顶的"拉什则"（藏语，山顶的意思）去朝拜，但是在藏民朝圣的路上和目的地，都可以看到汉族的花灯展览和社火表演；现在每年正月十五藏地隆重的酥油灯会，据说也大大受到了汉地正月十五元宵灯会的影响；在四川的一些藏区，过年时候也可以看到不少藏人家里的门上学汉人贴上对联，以求吉利；藏地在藏历年期间所流行的摔跤、投石、射箭等竞技活动据说跟蒙古文化的影响不无关系。因此，与异文化的不断交融也是藏历年习俗变迁的重要因素。

再加上藏地广袤，各个地区由于历史、地理、人文传承等方面的不同，致使藏历年的习俗也呈现出具有浓郁区域特色的样态，大大增加了藏文化的多样性。

而随着时间的推移，到了现代，人们过藏历年的习俗更是加入了不少现代生活元素。现在在藏区的大部分地方，从年二十九开始的一系列传统仪式和习俗，包括清洁、装饰、吃食和娱乐活动等都还会按照传统的程序进行，但同时譬如像准备的新年食物，既有传统的青稞、小麦、糌粑做的食物，也会买现代的美食佳酿和各种糖果，或者到外订餐在家吃团圆饭；娱乐方面既可以看到很多传统的庆祝方式，譬如围绕布达拉宫、大昭寺礼佛，身着节日盛装唱歌跳舞，举行各种竞技比赛和游戏，更可以看到人们看电视、唱"卡拉OK"，

The territory of Tibetan areas is broad, there are great differences in the aspects of history, geography, humanity heritage etc., which lead to diversified Tibetan New Year conventions with strong regional characteristics.

As time goes on, many modern life elements are added into Tibetan New Year celebration conventions in modern times. At present, most places in Tibetan areas have a series of traditional ceremonies and conventions since the twenty-ninth day, such as cleaning, decoration, eating foods and entertainment activities etc. Traditional procedures shall be followed, for example, foods which are prepared for New Year include traditional foods made in barley, wheat and Zanba, modern delicious food, fine wine and various kinds of sweets, or having family reunion meal outside; in terms of entertainment, we can see a lot of traditional celebration methods, for example, worshiping Buddhas around the Potala Palace and the Jokhang Temple, singing and dancing in splendid festival clothes, holding various kinds of athletic contests, we can see people watching TV, singing KaraOK and young people wearing fashionable and new-styled clothes, playing table tennis and playing modern dances pleasantly. In recent years, CCTV has broadcasted Spring Festival Gala Evening to celebrate Tibetan New Year like

Spring Festival Gala Evening watched on Spring Festival's eve in the Han ethnic region of China. Since Happy Song in Snowland broadcasted in 2009 was popular among common Tibetan people, and watching Tibetan New Year Gala Evening has become an indispensable entertainment of many Tibetans yearly.

In many places, it's popular for people to celebrate other festival ceremonies with Tibetan New Year together for greater happiness and better luck. For example, Tibetans around Qinghai Lake hold life ceremonies such as wedding, birthday celebration and cutting fetal hair etc. during New Year. Some places celebrate festivals such as Horse Racing Festival and Shoton Festival etc. with New Year. The integration of these activities has formed the ceremony of New Year Festival in modern sense.

Although some ceremonies or conventions have disappeared and decayed during the transition of Tibetan New Year having a history of one thousand years, the transition of history has endowed new

年轻人更会身着时髦新潮的服装，潇洒地玩桌球、跳现代舞蹈等。在最近几年，如同汉族地区在除夕的夜晚观看"春节联欢晚会"一样，CCTV同样为庆祝藏族的藏历年播出藏历新年的春节联欢晚会，自2009年播出的《雪域欢歌》受到藏地老百姓的喜爱以来，之后年年过藏历年，观看藏历新年的联欢晚会也成为不少藏族同胞不可或缺的一种娱乐方式。

在很多地方，现在人们还流行将一些其他的节庆仪式拉到藏历年来一起过，以图更加喜庆、吉祥。譬如青海环湖一带的藏族流行在拜年期间举行婚礼、过寿、剃胎发等人生礼仪的活动。还有些地方就把过年与赛马节、雪顿节等节日合并起来一起过。这些活动聚合起来一起就形成了现在意义上的年节仪式。

藏历年在千年历史的流转中传承至今，期间虽然有一些仪式或习俗已消失衰落，但历史的变迁也在不断给藏历年赋予新的含义和内容，让它形成今天这样一个内涵丰富而又具多样性的节庆文化。在今天，它不仅是藏族人民最值得庆贺和珍视的一笔文化财富，也是世界文化宝库当中不可多得的一笔财富。

implications and contents to Tibetan New Year constantly, and made it such a diversified festival celebration culture with rich connotations. At present, it is a cultural wealth which Tibetans congratulate and cherish and is a rare wealth in treasury of world culture.

References

[1] Liao Dongfan, *Four Seasons of Festival Celebration*, China Tibetology Publishing House, 2007.

[2] Liao Dongfan, *Tibetan Customs*, China Tibetology Publishing House, 2008.

[3] Shen Zonglian and Shengqi Liu, *Tibet and Tibetans*, China Tibetology Publishing House, 2006.

[4] Chen Liming and Xiaoyan Cao, *Tibetan Folk Culture*, China Tibetology Publishing House, 2003.

[5] Li Chunsheng, *Tibetan Festivals*, Chongqing Publishing House, 2007.

[6] Lin Jifu, *Tibetan Festival Culture*, Tibet People's Publishing House, 1993.

参考文献

[1] 廖东凡.节庆四季[M].北京：中国藏学出版社，2007。

[2] 廖东凡.藏地风俗[M].北京：中国藏学出版社，2008。

[3] 沈宗濂，柳陞祺.西藏与西藏人[M].北京：中国藏学出版社，2006。

[4] 陈立明，曹晓燕.西藏民俗文化[M].北京：中国藏学出版社，2003。

[5] 李春生.藏族年节[M].重庆：重庆出版社，2007。

[6] 林继富.西藏节日文化[M].拉萨：西藏人民出版社，1993。

《中国节庆文化》
丛书后记

　　上下五千年的悠久历史孕育了灿烂辉煌的中华文化。中国地域辽阔，民族众多，节庆活动丰富多彩，而如此众多的节庆活动就是一座座珍贵丰富的旅游资源宝藏。在中华民族漫长的历史中所形成的春节、清明、端午、中秋、重阳等众多传统节日和少数民族节日，是中华民族优秀传统文化的历史积淀，是中华民族精神和情感传承的重要载体，是维系祖国统一、民族团结、文化认同、社会和谐的精神纽带，是中华民族生生不息的不竭动力。

　　为了传播中华民族优秀传统文化，打造中国的优秀民族节庆品牌，中国人类学民族学研究会民族节庆专业委员会与安徽人民出版社合作，在国务

The Postscript of
Chinese Festival Culture Series

China has developed its splendid and profound culture during its long history of 5000 years. It has a vast territory, numerous ethnic groups as well as the colorful festivals. The rich festival activities have become the invaluable tourism resources. The traditional festivals, such as the Spring Festival, the Tomb-Sweeping Day, the Dragon Boat Festival, the Mid-Autumn Day and the Double-Ninth Festival as well as the festivals of ethnic minorities, are representing the excellent traditional culture of China and have become an important carrier bearing the spirits and emotions of the Chinese people, the spirit bond of the national reunification, national unity, cultural identity and social harmony, and an inexhaustible driving force for the development of the Chinese Nation.

In order to spread the excellent traditional culture of China and build the folk festival brand for our country, the Folk Festival Commission of the China Union of Anthropological and Ethnological Sciences (CUAES) has worked with the Anhui People's Publishing House to publish the *Chinese*

Festival Culture Series under the support from the State Council Information Office. For this purpose, the Folk Festival Commission has established the editorial board of the *Chinese Festival Culture Series*, by inviting Mr. Steven Wood Schmader, the president and CEO of the International Festival and Events Association (IFEA); Mr. Feng Jicai, the executive vice-president of China Federation of Literary and Art Circles; Mr. Zhou Mingfu, the vice-chairman of the China Union of Anthropological and Ethnological Sciences (CUAES); Mr. Huang Zhongcai, the deputy director of the politics research office of the National Ethnic Affairs Commission, and the secretary-general of the China Union of Anthropological and Ethnological Sciences (CUAES); Ms. Wu Cuiying , the director of the Cultural Promotion Department of the National Ethnic Affairs Commission as consultants; Li Song, the director of the Folk Literature and Art Development Center of the Ministry of Culture as the chief editor; and 16 famous scholars as the members to organize, plan, select and determine the topics and determine the authors. After the establishment of the board, 50 famous experts and scholars in the field of festivals and the festival planners with extensive experiences have been invited to jointly edit the series.

The planning of the *Chinese Festival Culture Series* is to promote the traditional Chinese culture, explore the local and unique cultures, showcase the charms of the festivals of the Chinese Nation,

院新闻办公室的大力支持下，决定联合出版大型系列丛书——《中国节庆文化》丛书。为此，民族节庆专委会专门成立了《中国节庆文化》丛书编纂委员会，邀请了国际节庆协会（IFEA）主席兼首席执行官史蒂文·施迈德先生、中国文联执行副主席冯骥才先生、中国人类学民族学研究会常务副会长周明甫先生、国家民委政研室副主任兼中国人类学民族学研究会秘书长黄忠彩先生、国家民委文宣司司长武翠英女士等担任顾问，由文化部民族民间文艺发展中心主任李松担任主编，十六位知名学者组成编委会，负责丛书的组织策划、选题确定、体例拟定和作者的甄选。随后，组委会在全国范围内，遴选了五十位节庆领域知名专家学者以及有着丰富实操经验的节庆策划师共同编著。

策划《中国节庆文化》丛书，旨在弘扬中国传统文化，挖掘本土文化和独特文化，展示中华民族的节庆魅力，展现绚丽多姿的民俗风情，打造节庆城市形象。本丛书以对中国节庆文化感兴趣的中外读者为对象，以节庆活动为载体，向世界推广中国的传统文化和现代文化，让中国走向世界，让世界更了解中国。编委会要求每位参与编写者，力争做到理论性与实践性兼备，集专业性与通俗性于一体。

目前推出的是第一辑《春之节》，其编纂工作自2012年4月启动，2013年6月完成。期间编委会先后六次召开了专题会议，就丛书编纂体例、书目大纲、初稿、译稿与作者及译者进行研讨，共同修改完善书稿和译稿；就丛书的装帧设计、编辑风格、出版发行计划与出版社进行协商，集思广益，提高丛书的文化品位。

《春之节》共十册，分别介绍了中华大地上农历一月至三月有代表性的十个民族节庆，包括春节、元宵节、二月二、三月三、清明节、牡丹节、藏历年、壮族蚂𧑓节、苗

express the gorgeous and colorful folk customs and create a festival image for cities. The target consumers of the series are the readers both at home and abroad who are interested in the festivals of China, and the purpose of the series is to promote the traditional culture and modern culture of China to the world and make the world know China in a better way by using the festivals as medium. The editorial board requests the editors shall integrate the theories into practice and balance the expertise and the popularity.

At present, the first part of the series will be published, namely the *Festivals in Spring*, and the editorial work of this part has been started in April, 2012 and completed in June, 2013. During this period of time, the editorial board has held six meetings to discuss with the authors and translators in terms of the compiling styles, outlines, first draft and translation to improve the draft and translation; and to consult with the publishing house in terms of the graphic design, editorial style and publishing schedule to improve the cultural quality of the series.

The first part *Festivals in Spring* is composed of 10 volumes to introduce 10 folk festivals of China from the first month to the third month of the Chinese Calendar, including the Spring Festival, the Lantern Festival, the Festival of February of the Second, the Festival of March the Third, the Tomb-Sweeping Day, the Peony Festival, the

Tibetan Calendar New Year, the Maguai Festival of the Zhuang People, the Sister Rice Festival, and the Saizhuang Festival of the Yi Ethnic Group. Each festival is introduced in detail to analyse its origin, development, distribution, customs, overseas dissemination and major activities, showing the readers a colorful picture about the Chinese festivals.

This series are the product of the cooperation between the Folk Festival Commission and the Anhui People's Publishing House. Anhui People's Publishing House is the first publishing house of its kind in Anhui Province, which has a history of more than 60 years, and has been in the leading position in terms of foreign publication. The Folk Festival Commission is the only organization at the national level in the field of the research of the Chinese festivals, which has rich expert resources and local festival resources. The series have integrated the advantageous resources of both parties. We will be delighted and gratified to see that the series could promote the foreign dissemination of the Chinese culture, promote the inheritance and preservation of the traditional and folk cultures, express the cultural charms of China and build the festival brand and image of China.

In deep meditation, the *Chinese Festival Culture Series* bears the wisdoms and knowledge of all of its authors and the great effort of the editors, and

族姊妹节、彝族赛装节等，对每个节日的起源与发展、空间流布、节日习俗、海外传播、现代主要活动形式等分别进行了详细的介绍和深度的挖掘，呈现给读者的将是一幅绚丽多彩的中华节庆文化画卷。

这套丛书的出版，是民族节庆专业委员会和安徽人民出版社合作的结晶。安徽人民出版社是安徽省最早的出版社，有六十余年的建社历史，在对外传播方面走在全国出版社的前列；民族节庆专业委员会是我国节庆研究领域唯一的国家级社团，拥有丰富的专家资源和地方节庆资源。这套丛书的出版，实现了双方优势资源的整合。丛书的面世，若能对推动中国文化的对外传播，促进传统民族文化的传承与保护，展示中华民族的文化魅力，塑造节庆的品牌与形象有所裨益，我们将甚感欣慰。

掩卷沉思，《中国节庆文化》丛书凝聚着诸位作者的智慧和学养，倾注着编纂者的心血和付出，也诠释着中华民族文化的灿烂与辉煌。在此，真诚感谢各位编委会成员、丛书作者、译者、出版社工作人员付出的辛勤劳动，以及各界朋友对丛书编纂工作的鼎力支持！希望各位读者对丛书多提宝贵意见，以便我们进一步完善后续作品，将更加璀璨的节庆文化呈现在世界面前。

《中国节庆文化》
丛书编委会
2013年12月

explains the splendid cultures of the Chinese Nation. We hereby sincerely express our gratitude to the members of the board, the authors, the translators, and the personnel in the publishing house for their great effort and to all friends from all walks of the society for their support. We hope you can provide your invaluable opinions for us to further promote the following work so as to show the world our excellent festival culture.

Editorial Board of
Chinese Festival Culture Series
December, 2013